M000318217

HAUNTED
DEARBORN COUNTY,
INDIANA

MARY ELLEN QUIGLEY AND REBECCA D. WILHELM

HAUNTED
America

Published by Haunted America
A Division of The History Press
Charleston, SC
www.historypress.com

Copyright © 2023 by Mary Ellen Quigley and Rebecca D. Wilhelm
All rights reserved

All images from the collection of Rebecca D. Wilhelm.

First published 2023

ISBN 9781467153331

Library of Congress Control Number: 2023934799

Notice: The information in this book is true and complete to the best of our knowledge. It is offered without guarantee on the part of the authors or The History Press. The authors and The History Press disclaim all liability in connection with the use of this book.

All rights reserved. No part of this book may be reproduced or transmitted in any form whatsoever without prior written permission from the publisher except in the case of brief quotations embodied in critical articles and reviews.

This book is dedicated to Earl and Hope,
who have always loved a good ghost story.
Love, Mama

This book is dedicated to my nieces and nephews for always cheering me on
and encouraging me to be a better person.
Love, Aunt Mary

CONTENTS

INTRODUCTION

C ome along with us as we explore a few of the hauntings from Dearborn County, Indiana. What is it exactly that makes this place so special? There is an amazing history here. When researching the history, folklore and ghostly legends from the area, one thing that stands out is the ability of the people here to persevere through countless tragedies and hardships. This is what sets Dearborn County apart from the rest.

Dearborn County sits along the Ohio and Kentucky borders in the southeast part of the state of Indiana. This location gives Dearborn County a unique place in the state. Depending on the location in the county, it is about a thirty- or forty-minute drive from downtown Cincinnati and about a twenty-minute drive to the Greater Cincinnati/Northern Kentucky Airport. This makes the area a desirable spot for those who need to live near a big city but like the small-town feel that the communities of the area provide.

The Ohio River proudly flows along the edge of the southeast portion of the county, dividing it from Ohio and Kentucky. The river has always been a huge source of income for the county, especially in its early days and foundation. Riverboats and Dearborn County go hand in hand. Trading in the area was made possible because Lawrenceburg and Aurora are in proximity to the Ohio River.

Settlers from the eastern United States, looking for a better life, began to migrate into the Ohio Valley in the late eighteenth century. These people began settling into the areas we now know as Washington, Center and Lawrenceburg Townships. Many people today do not realize that

The Guilford covered bridge, built in 1879 by A.M. Kennedy & Sons, is the last covered bridge in Dearborn County.

a Revolutionary War battle occurred along the Ohio River near what is present-day Aurora and in the area that is now River View Cemetery.

These early settlers came to Dearborn County looking for rich farmland and a new beginning. Records show that the Federal Land Office, which was located in Cincinnati, started showing people registering their land in the area beginning in 1801. According to the Dearborn County government website, these early pioneer settlers tended to make homesteads in "the lower creek valleys and along the Ohio River bottomland."

In 1803, Dearborn County became the seventy-seventh county in the state of Indiana. It was founded by then governor William Henry Harrison, who later became the ninth president of the United States. Harrison was the governor of the Indiana territory at that time. Harrison would become famous for having the shortest presidency in U.S. history to date. Harrison caught a cold while giving his inauguration speech in the rain. His cold would prove to be fatal when it later turned into pneumonia. Harrison served only thirty-one days in office. Harrison named Dearborn County after General Henry Dearborn. At that time, Henry Dearborn was the secretary of war under President Thomas Jefferson.

A view of the Ohio River taken from Aurora, Indiana. The Ohio River has been vital to the success of Dearborn County.

Hay bale on a farm along County Line Road in Moores Hill, Indiana. Agriculture played a large part in founding the area.

A farm in Wilmington, Indiana. In 1910, there were over two thousand farms located in the county.

Interestingly enough, the county is nicknamed "the gore." *Gore* means "a triangular piece of pie" or "a slice." The nickname is because Dearborn, Franklin, Ohio, Randolph, Switzerland, Union, Wayne and Fayette were originally one county and considered to be a part of the Ohio Territory. It looked like a gore. The seven counties broke apart in 1811 and became separate, with Switzerland County being the last to break away and form its own county in 1814. According to the Dearborn County government website, the present boundaries we know as Dearborn County today were established back in 1845.

Dearborn County consists of fourteen townships. The townships are Caesar Creek, Center, Clay, Harrison, Hogan, Jackson, Kelso, Lawrenceburg, Logan, Manchester, Miller, Sparta, Washington and York. Washington was the last one to form, in 1852.

In July 1863, the Civil War came to Dearborn County and left a mark on history, as well as a few legends. Confederate general John Hunt Morgan and his troops invaded the county that summer. Morgan's Raid, as it historically has been called, was carried out by a group of 2,500 Confederate men. The raid began in Tennessee and moved through

Kentucky, invading Indiana and Ohio. Throughout their path, Morgan's raiders destroyed railroad bridges by burning them down. The men also stole about four thousand horses and wreaked havoc and terror on the communities of Manchester, Jackson, Kelso, Logan and Harrison Townships. The madness of this raid lasted for a total of forty-six days before Morgan was finally captured in Ohio. When it was all over, it was estimated that about $1 million in damages was reported. Some feel that Morgan's raid left a mark on the area that was never erased.

Over the years, illness has also been a major factor in the sorrows of the county. According to a Greencastle, Indiana newspaper, spotted fever made an appearance in Dearborn County in 1866, and it took many lives. The fever was said to kill a person within two hours of coming down with symptoms. It mostly affected Miller Township.

The county was mostly agricultural in its early days. To put in perspective just how big a part agriculture played in the founding of the area, in 1910, there were over two thousand farms located in the county. According to county records, the average farm had at least eighty-three acres of land.

There are three cities located in Dearborn County: Aurora, Greendale and Lawrenceburg. Lawrenceburg, the county seat and the largest city, has held that distinction since 1803. Lawrenceburg was founded in 1802. It was founded by Samuel Vance, James Hamilton and Benjamin Chambers. Vance named the city to honor his wife; Lawrence was her maiden name.

Aurora, Indiana, would follow Lawrenceburg sixteen years later, establishing itself as a city in 1819. Aurora is named after the Roman goddess of dawn. Aurora is well known for being the final resting place of blues guitarist Lonnie Mack, who was raised in the area. It is also known for the Greek Revival–style Hillforest mansion, a picturesque downtown and the legend of the glowing grave at River View Cemetery.

Greendale, Indiana, is the newest of the Dearborn County cities. It was founded in 1852 but was not recorded as a city until 1883. It's believed that the city took its name from the Greendale Cemetery, which was established in 1862. It is also well known for the Schenley distillery.

There was only a brief period from 1836 to 1844 when Wilmington served as the county seat. The first courthouse was constructed in 1810 and was destroyed by a fire. The present-day courthouse was built in 1870 and has a long history of sad stories and at least one suicide occurring there. The courthouse has long been thought to be a haunted location.

When you walk along the path at Lesko Park in Aurora or the levee walk in Lawrenceburg, the Ohio River gives you a sense of peace and calm.

The Lawrenceburg, Indiana town clock at the levee on High Street, erected in 2002 for the city's bicentennial celebration.

Many people are drawn to the area because of the beauty of the river. However, some believe this water is the source of much of the paranormal phenomena. Water is believed by many cultures to be a good conductor of ghosts and spirits. Spirits are said to be able to move through the water and to use water as a pathway between their world and our own.

While beautiful, the Ohio River has been a source of much heartache since the founding of the area. Dearborn County has seen many floods over the years. In fact, the Shawnee Native Americans cautioned early settlers against building in the area around the river. The worst flood on record occurred on January 26, 1937. This was when the Ohio River reached a height of eighty feet. To put this in perspective, it was thirty feet over the flood stage. This flood affected Dearborn County and the entire Ohio Valley region from Pittsburgh, Pennsylvania, to Cairo, Illinois. When it was through, the flooding caused the death of 385 people across the affected states and almost $500 million in damages and losses. There are homes in Lawrenceburg where mud from the Ohio River still clings to the attic rafters as a testament to how high the floodwaters once rose.

A view of Second Street in Aurora, Indiana, where several buildings date to the early 1800s.

The Dearborn County Courthouse in Lawrenceburg, Indiana. The first courthouse was built in 1810 and rebuilt in 1870 due to fire.

Lawrenceburg's response to the 1937 flood was to build a levee. Today, the city has installed flood doors and walls that protect the town from a tragedy of that magnitude ever occurring again. Aurora has seen several major flood occurrences since the 1937 flood. A severe flood occurred in 1997 when the river reached a height of 64.7 feet. During another flood in 2018, the river reached a height of 61.0 feet.

This is a county that has seen it all. Plagued with deaths, illness, murders, a Revolutionary War battle, the Civil War and the many floods over the years, Dearborn County has seen its fair share of tragedy. Through it all, the people of this county persevere, and perhaps that is why many are long gone but refuse to be silent.

1

HILLFOREST MANSION HAUNTINGS

As you turn onto Main Street in downtown Aurora and climb the hill to Fifth Street, it would be hard to miss the magnificent yellow house that has sat atop the hill overlooking the town for the past 167 years. Surrounded by sycamore trees and a dash of mystery, the Hillforest Mansion is synonymous with Aurora and Dearborn County history. Built between 1853 and 1855 for Thomas Gaff and his family, Hillforest Mansion has stood the test of time and has left a mark on the town that few other locations in the area can boast of.

The home, originally named Forest Hill, was built by the famous architect Isaiah Rogers, who is well known as the father of the modern hotel. Many of Rogers's buildings have sadly been lost to time over the years, and Hillforest is special because it is one of the few remaining examples of his architecture that is left in the United States. It has also largely gone untouched, having not faced any major alterations from Rogers's original design of the mansion.

According to an article on the Cincinnati USA website, Rogers built the Thomas Gaff home in the Italian Renaissance style, "completely symmetrical and characterized by broad overhangs, ornately carved brackets, arched windows, and graceful balconies and porches." This may seem like an oddly elaborate design for a home in a small town along the Ohio River. However, the owner of this estate, Thomas Gaff, had a track record of thinking big and did the same with the construction of his house.

Thomas Gaff was born in Edinburgh, Scotland, on July 8, 1808. He immigrated to the United States with his parents in 1811, when he was three

Aurora, Indiana's Hillforest Mansion at 213 Fifth Street. The house was the Gaff family home from 1855 until 1926.

years old. The Gaff family moved around a lot during Gaff's childhood. According to historical documents, the family lived in Upstate New York, Brooklyn and New Jersey before finally settling in Pennsylvania, where they began their business adventures.

Gaff was what you would consider a self-made businessman who, along with his brothers, James and John, developed several successful business interests. The Gaff brothers started out in the paper-making, storekeeping and distillery businesses in Philadelphia. Just as the brothers were starting to get successful, disaster struck with the Panic of 1837.

The Panic of 1837 was a time of economic hardship that many historians believe was the result of the financial policies of President Andrew Jackson. According to the Library of Congress website, Jackson believed that the United States bank held too much control over citizens "by exercising too much control over credit and economic opportunity, and he succeeded in shutting it down." This affected not only the United States and Great Britain but markets all over Europe and China as well. The tax on alcohol increased. Grain that was needed to make liquor became difficult to obtain. Neither of these situations was good for the Gaffs' Philadelphia distillery. This marked a dark period in history, with a depression that lasted until the mid-1840s. The United States did not fully come out of the depression until the gold rush in 1848.

Hit hard by this period of economic depression, the Gaff brothers decided to sell their distillery business in Pennsylvania and move to Aurora, Indiana, for a chance at a fresh start. According to the National Register of Historic Places Registration Form completed in 1992, the Gaff brothers were offered a lucrative tax incentive and land if they would bring their distillery business to Aurora. According to the paperwork filed for Hillforest's nomination, James was the first to arrive in Aurora, followed by Thomas in 1843 and, finally, John.

The Gaff brothers started their business in Indiana by running a dry goods storefront and a shipping business in a building at the corner of Judiciary and Second Streets. They also lived in an apartment above their storefront. Interestingly, the Gaff family consisted of the three Gaff brothers; their mother, who was a widow; and their three sisters. As the sisters and the brothers married, they left the cramped upstairs apartment. However, Thomas; his wife, Sarah; his mother, Margaret; and three daughters continued to live in the apartment until Hillforest was completed in 1855. This building where the dry goods store was located still stands and is used as apartments today. There is also a mystery associated with this building, which is told in a later chapter of this book.

The Gaff brothers eventually made their money in whiskey and beer with the start of the Thomas and James Gaff Distillery, which was located on Hogan Creek in two warehouse buildings in 1843 that are still standing today on Importing Street. They also began a brewery called the Crescent Brewery across from Lesko Park along State Road 56 in Aurora. The remnants of a retaining wall to the building and the tunnels used to store beer, and keep it cold, can still be seen along Market Street today. The Gaffs transported their liquor all over the United States, across Europe and "as far away as Australia," according an article about the brewery on the Lewis and Clark National Historic Trail Experience website. The Gaffs' Crescent Brewery produced a beer that was called Aurora Lager Beer. At one point in the 1870s, the Gaffs' Crescent Brewery was the largest brewery in the entire state of Indiana.

The very first telephone in Aurora, Indiana, was installed in the Gaffs' warehouse in 1869 on Importing Street, and it provided a telephone connection from the warehouse to a company called the Henry Winthrope Smith Co. in Cincinnati, Ohio. Today, you will find the Great Crescent Brewery, deriving its name from the Gaffs' original brewery, located in one of the Gaffs' warehouses. A recycling center is located across the street in the other warehouse.

One thing that stands out about Thomas Gaff is that he was remarkable at exploring business opportunities and making them successful. Outside of the aforementioned businesses, he also had a silver mine in Nevada, two Louisiana plantations, a jewelry store in Cincinnati and a fleet of steamships. His steamships included the *Diana*, the *Mary Pell*, the *Eclipse*, the *J.W. Gaff* and, most famously, the *Forest Queen*.

The *Forest Queen* was commandeered during the Civil War. General William Tecumseh Sherman used the steamship as his headquarters during the Battle of Vicksburg. The *Forest Queen* was eventually burned in the Mississippi River at St. Louis in 1863 by the Confederate army. According to Hillforest Mansion staff, Thomas Gaff never received money for the loss of the ship from the U.S. government.

One of his most interesting business ventures was the creation of one of the first dry breakfast cereals in the country, called Cerealine, which was produced at his mill in Columbus, Indiana. This breakfast cereal predated Kellogg's Corn Flakes and was one of the top cereals sold across the country at this time. Thomas Gaff and his brother James had also partnered with Julius Fleischmann for a new type of yeast, helping found the Fleischmann yeast company in Cincinnati. In the beginning, the business was known as the Gaff Fleischmann Co.

Main Street Aurora, Indiana, with a view of the Presbyterian church and town clock. The clock was a gift from the Gaff family.

Hillforest Mansion was built overlooking the Ohio River, which makes sense considering the importance of shipping and riverboats in Gaff's businesses. The semicircular design mimics the look of an old riverboat, and the third-floor belvedere resembles a pilothouse. The top of the house has an observation room where Gaff used to watch his steamboats as they traveled along the river. It is thought that Gaff would play cards and meet with his friends in this observation room.

There is a long-told legend involving the narrow, steep steps leading to the observation room. It was thought for many years that the steps were purposefully built narrow to ensure that ladies of the day could not go up the steps since their skirts or dresses would keep them from being able to navigate the steps safely. According to a current docent of the mansion, this has been thought to be false.

Despite being a remarkable businessman, Thomas Gaff was also someone who was very involved with the building of the town of Aurora. According to the Hillforest website, Gaff was responsible for backing the town's first utility company, the Aurora Gas and Coke Company, and founding the First National Bank of Aurora. Gaff served as president of the bank.

According to the Hillforest Victorian House Museum website, Gaff also helped to "organize Aurora's public school system, served on the City Council with his brother James, incorporated River View Cemetery, and, with his brothers, bought for Aurora a fire engine and town clock." Thomas Gaff was the very first school board member of Aurora's public schools. He was so concerned with education because his own children had to be tutored at home since the town did not have a good public education available. It was important to Gaff to correct that.

Although Gaff was so instrumental in founding the town, a visitor to Hillforest Mansion will find that there are no known paintings, photos or drawings of Thomas Gaff. Only a portrait of his brother James and sister-in-law Rachel is hanging in his former home. This is a strange finding indeed.

Why there are no known photos, paintings or portraits of Thomas Gaff is just one of the many legends and secrets that this mansion holds. There is a long-held rumor around Aurora that when Gaff passed away in Cincinnati on April 25, 1884, he did so in a brothel. Legend is that Sarah Gaff was so angry, upset and heartbroken over Gaff's passing and the location of his death that she burned every portrait there ever was of him. A former docent to the home reported that on the anniversary of Gaff's death, smoke can be smelled and the sounds of a woman weeping and sobbing uncontrollably can be heard.

There is only one other portrait painting of the family in the mansion besides James and Rachel. In the master bedroom, you will find a portrait of Caroline Gaff, who passed away at age fifteen before the family moved into Hillforest. Sadly, she was only three days short of turning sixteen when she passed from scarlet fever in the family's apartment above the dry goods store. A common practice of this period was to commission a painting of the deceased as a way to remember how they looked. The painting hanging in the master bedroom was made after Caroline's death as a way for the family to remember her.

The portrait of Caroline is where another tale of the Hillforest hauntings begins. According to the mansion's former director Cindy Schuette, strange things started happening when the portrait was donated back to the house several years ago. One of the first things the staff noticed was the bedspread in the master bedroom always being disturbed as if someone had been lying in it. There was also an uneasy feeling in the room, as if you were being followed or watched. Many believe it could be the spirit of Caroline visiting her old home.

Then there is the legend of the apparition of a girl that has been seen in the upstairs master bedroom. A former docent of the mansion claimed that there were several times when visitors would comment and ask about the teenage girl in period clothing seen in the upstairs bedroom. The docent would inform the visitor that there was no one of that description on the staff.

The most common occurrence in the home that began after the painting arrived is the doorbell ringing with no one on the other side. Lights were also known to turn on and begin flickering or go out completely. Staff also sometimes heard voices. One such experience involved a local repairman working in the bathroom who heard someone call out his name. After investigating, he found that there was no one else on that level of the home.

Cindy Schuette shared the strange incident of hearing a woman's voice yell out "yoohoo" one morning as she walked up the stairs to her office. The rest of the staff had not arrived yet, so no one else was in the building. A former docent, who wishes to remain anonymous, was in the building alone one afternoon when they heard the sound of crying and smelled smoke. As they were getting ready to call for help, they realized no actual fire was happening. There have been multiple encounters like this, and most volunteers of Hillforest have a story involving the unexplained.

The staircase has been the location of several reported hauntings at the mansion, although the hauntings have been attributed to a couple of ghosts. Besides Caroline, it is thought that Mr. Gaff's grandson, Charles Gaff Howe, or Naughty Charlie, as he was called, could be one of the culprits. Naughty Charlie was a bit of a prankster and was known for playing tricks on people and causing a ruckus in the household. An upstairs closet still bears his name etched into the wood. A well-known story that docents like to tell visitors to the mansion is about Naughty Charlie riding his horse, a pony, up the house's main staircase and out of the second-floor back door. Some of the more playful hauntings, such as items being moved around, are often thought to be Naughty Charlie playing his famous pranks again.

Former staff at Hillforest have also claimed to have seen the figure of a woman on the main staircase and in the main doorway over the years. Orbs are often seen on the staircase and have been caught in many photographs over the years. Weddings are held at the mansion, and it is not uncommon for orbs to show up in wedding photos or for people to report odd happenings during an event at the mansion.

In October 2020, Rebecca and Hope Wilhelm conducted an interview for their podcast, *Hoosier Myths and Legends*, and during the interview, they experienced their own encounter with the staircase orbs. As they were taking a tour of the home with a docent, Sussanah Ulrich, they stopped briefly to take some pictures of the elaborate design of the staircase. Ulrich was sharing how she was married at Hillforest and threw her bouquet from a certain spot on the stairs. When looking at the pictures, later on, a definite blue orb appears to be following them on their way up.

Another experience happened while sitting in the family parlor, talking with the ladies about the history of the home. When the staff members began to share some ghost stories about the home, a loud bang came from the upper level of the house. It sounded like a door slamming shut. There were only five people in the house at the time, and all of them were sitting in the parlor.

In 2020, Korrinn Wood posted a video on her YouTube page where she visited the mansion and recorded footage of the beautiful architecture and décor. Korrinn didn't notice anything out of the ordinary during her time there until she reviewed the footage she had recorded later. Not only are there multiple orbs caught throughout the video, but Wood also caught footage of the flickering lights and a disembodied voice that seems to be calling her name. She had no idea the place was considered to be haunted until she contacted a local ghost-hunting group who confirmed the experience she had.

Another popular legend about the mansion is that you can sometimes hear the sound of a young boy crying for his mother. This has been caught on recordings by a local ghost-hunting group. It is believed that this may be the voice of Thomas Gaff Mitchell, a grandson who passed away in the mansion from illness at the age of three. Several docents have also reported hearing a little boy crying over the years.

It is also said that you can hear the sounds of Sarah Gaff sobbing on the anniversary of Thomas Gaff's death. Although, the sounds of the sobbing could also be for another reason. The Gaffs' adult daughter Vienna passed away in Louisiana at the age of twenty-nine. Thomas Gaff owned a plantation there and asked Vienna and her husband to oversee it. Vienna was bitten by a mosquito and died from a virus it carried. The mansion staff has records of letters written by one of Vienna's sisters explaining how the Gaffs mourned Vienna's death by walking the halls of Hillforest crying out for her. In the letters, it's said that Thomas Gaff cried out for Vienna over and over again and walked the upstairs hallway for many nights. He felt guilt over her death because he felt it would not have happened had

Aurora's Hillforest Mansion with a view of the signs advertising upcoming events. Hillforest hosts many popular events throughout the year.

he not asked her to go to Louisiana. Could the crying be the Gaffs still mourning their daughter's passing all these years later?

In 1926, Hillforest was sold to William Stark, who owned a local furniture company, the Cochran Chair Company. Hillforest was famous while the Starks owned the home. Mrs. Stark was known to decorate the home elaborately, and she made newspapers of the time for her beautiful décor. The VFW purchased the home in 1948. The organization operated it as a place for veterans to come home after World War II, where they had apartments upstairs that returning soldiers could rent and live in with their families.

The home has since operated as a museum after it was saved by Esther Roach and a group of concerned citizens back in 1956. Hillforest has been open to the public as a local history museum ever since. People come from all over the country to view its beauty. It hosts weddings, multiple community events and a popular Murder Mystery Dinner held every October. This beautiful home has been an important part of the Dearborn County community since it was built, and hopefully, it will continue to be so for many years to come.

2

THE GLOWING GRAVE
OF RIVER VIEW CEMETERY

The historic River View Cemetery in Aurora, Indiana, is arguably one of the prettiest burial grounds in all of southeastern Indiana. The cemetery was established in 1869 and was designed in the Victorian style by architect William Tinsley. Tinsley is well known for being the architect of the original college building for Indiana University. Tinsley has a long history of building institutional buildings throughout the Midwest.

As you pull onto the cemetery drive, located off of Laughery Creek Road, you will first notice the gorgeous massive oak trees that line each of the winding pathways. As you drive around the well-maintained thirty-acre property, it is apparent the peaceful surroundings are a beautiful resting place for the thirteen thousand souls buried here. Looking at these lovely grounds makes it hard for anyone to believe that this hallowed ground is the home of a mystery and the site of an American Revolution battle.

One does not think of Indiana when one thinks of the American Revolution, but a battle did occur on the present-day site of River View Cemetery. Lochry's defeat, also referred to as the Lochry massacre, occurred here on August 24, 1781. The battle was between Great Britain and the colonists. No British were killed, but thirty-seven colonists were slain, and over sixty were captured. The spot where the massacre occurred is marked with signs on the cemetery grounds, which you will see as you drive around the property.

River View Cemetery is well known today for being the final resting place of the legendary blues and rock-n-roll guitarist Lonnie Mack. Mack grew

River View Cemetery entrance in Aurora, Indiana. This cemetery, founded in 1869, is the site of many ghostly tales.

up in Aurora, Indiana. The cemetery also made national news in 1989 when Mrs. Aurora Shuck, the wife of an Aurora businessman, was laid to rest in her red 1975 Cadillac. However, if you find yourself at River View Cemetery late at night, something strange might catch your eye. Over the last eighty-one years, many people have reported catching a glimpse of a glowing headstone among the gravestones late at night.

There have been many theories about the mysterious light. Some legends claim that it is only the lights from cars on the nearby road and their reflections. Others believe the glow is a security light reflecting off the gravestone. Another legend says that it may be from some unknown additive when the cement was poured for the stone. The strangest theory is that the grave is glowing because of whose grave it is.

The grave that is said to glow belongs to Virginius "Dink" Carter, who is possibly one of the most cold-blooded killers that Dearborn County, Indiana, has ever seen. On Friday, May 16, 1941, Dink Carter made national headlines when he killed his wife's family on their Laughery Creek Road farm, just four miles outside of the Aurora City limits. As you can imagine, this mass murder was big news in 1941. The May 22, 1941 *Aurora Bulletin* newspaper reported that this crime was "the most frightful crime in the history of Dearborn County." This remains true over eighty years later. Things like that did not happen in Dearborn County.

Carter murdered five members of his wife's family in cold blood. Among the victims were his father and mother-in-law, Johnston and Nina Agrue, and both of their sons, William and Leo. Leo was Carter's wife Leona's twin brother. The youngest of Carter's victims was little Mary Elizabeth Breeden, the granddaughter of Nina and Johnston Agrue. She was the child of the Agrues' daughter Ethel Agrue Wiant of Chicago and William Breeden of Lawrenceburg.

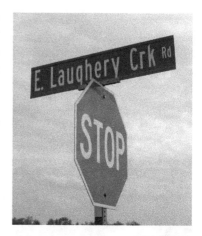

Laughery Creek Road sign in Aurora, Indiana. Along this road is the location of one of Indiana's most notorious murders.

Mary Elizabeth was staying with her grandparents that spring because of her parents' estrangement. According to different newspaper accounts, she was only eleven or twelve years old.

The bodies would not be discovered until the next day. On Saturday, May 17, neighbor Harvey Sellers and his son William grew concerned when they noticed that the Agrues' cows had not been milked and they were in an alfalfa field that morning. Alfalfa is dangerous to cattle and can cause bloat in cows. Harvey knew that Johnston Agrue would not have turned the cattle loose to eat in the alfalfa field. The family's horses were also out loose and roaming along a nearby hillside. Later, the Sellerses noticed the cows gathering at the barn. Being a good neighbor and knowing that this was all out of the ordinary, Harvey got his son William and went to quickly alert Johnson Agrue. Unfortunately, instead, a grisly sight awaited them.

Upon entering the family farm, the Sellerses first found the body of William Agrue. As they made their way to the house, they saw the body of little Mary Elizabeth in the barn. The Sellerses quickly left the property, horrified by what they had seen. They knew they had to call for help quickly, but there was no telephone at the Agrue farm or at their own farm. They went to another neighboring farm that had a telephone to call for the sheriff.

When law enforcement first arrived at the Agrue farm, they believed that the gruesome scene that lay before them was a robbery that had gone wrong. Dearborn County sheriff William Winegard first thought that robbery was a motive when deputies found a trunk in the upstairs of the Agrue home had been broken into. The axe that was used to bust the lock was lying next to it. When Sheriff Winegards spoke to the widow of William Agrue, he found out that the trunk had contained one hundred dollars in cash that was now missing. There was also a shotgun belonging to Leo Agrue that was missing. Deputies believed that the missing gun was the murder weapon since all of the victims were killed by a shotgun shot to their head or neck. The shotgun would later be found in the hollow of a tree on the Agrue farm property.

Sheriff Winegard knew right away that the murderer had to have known the family. Nina Agrue was killed while she was preparing the family dinner that fateful afternoon. When deputies entered the home, they could see that food was still on the stove and on the table. The *Aurora Bulletin* showed a picture of the family dinner table in the Thursday, May 22, 1941 newspaper. In the photograph, you can see that there was an additional place setting. The table was set for six people, meaning that Mrs. Agrue had known the killer. Eventually, a truck driver named Charles Campbell from Aurora came forward and told police that he had given Carter a ride out to the Agrue farm from Aurora on that fateful Friday. Campbell saw Carter thumbing for a ride on Third Street and dropped him off on Laughery Creek Road not far from the farm.

When Carter was first arrested, he told the deputies that he was illiterate and did not even know how to write his own name. At first, he denied committing the murders. Carter was given a lie detector test, but Captain Walter C. Eckhardt announced that the test was "fruitless." Carter ended up confessing to the murders in a signed confession after about fifty hours of intensive questioning. Carter was taken to the jail in Brookville, Indiana, to protect him from lynch mobs.

Over the years, there has been speculation about why Carter would do such a thing. The local newspapers reported that Carter claimed a long history of "family hatred" was a reason for the murder. Newspapers from the time quoted then Dearborn County sheriff William Winegard as saying that Carter confessed to having had a "grudge against his brothers-in-law." Witnesses at the trial spoke of a long-held feud between the two Agrue boys, Johnston Agrue and Dink Carter.

A 1941 *Indy Star* article quoted Carter's signed confession. In the confession, Carter admitted that "Leo and Willie Agrue hated me, and I killed them, later shot their father, Johnston Agrue, then the mother and lastly, the granddaughter, Mary Elizabeth Breeden." Carter chillingly described in the confession how he carried out the killings. The confession was written out for him, and he signed with a large X. Carter truly was illiterate and could not write his own name.

In the confession, he admitted to hitching a ride with Charles Campbell from downtown Aurora, on Third Street, about half of the way to the farm. He asked Campbell to park along Laughery Creek Road and then walked the rest of the way. Carter arrived at the house, where he entered and spoke first to Nina Agrue, who was washing dishes. He then asked her where Willie and Leo were. She told Carter that the boys were on the hill planting corn. He walked out of the house in search of them.

Carter walked up to the hill and confronted the Agrue boys. A struggle ensued, which ended with Carter getting Leo's shotgun from him. He first shot Leo, and then when Willie ran, he shot him at about two hundred yards. After calmly shooting both men in cold blood, he walked back to the house. Mrs. Agrue and Mary Elizabeth chatted with him for a little bit, not knowing what had just occurred. After a few minutes, Carter went out to meet Johnston Agrue at the hollow and shot him twice in the pathway between the holler and the house. After this, Carter went back into the house, where Mrs. Agrue asked him what the matter was. Nina had heard the shots fired that had killed both of her sons. Carter then shot Mrs. Agrue in the kitchen when she turned around. He told Mary Elizabeth to come with him, and she refused, saying she was going out to the barn instead. Carter took her to the barn, and the *Aurora Bulletin* quoted him as saying, "It was there I shot her."

According to old newspaper articles, it appears that Carter seemed to have been a troubled individual long before he met the Agrue family. The papers reported that Carter was married a total of four times. His first wife was named Nellie Mason, and they married in 1924, divorcing a short time later. He later married a lady by the name of Rosetta Willick in 1929, and that marriage also ended in a divorce. He had no children with either of these women.

After his first two divorces, Dink Carter's life seemed to take a nosedive. According to the Indiana State Police in a Greensburg newspaper article from 1941, Carter's problems with the law began in 1929. The *Greensburg Daily Reporter* noted that he was arrested for stealing a car and was sentenced to the Indiana State Reformatory. One jail stint just was not enough for Carter.

Carter also apparently spent some time in the Kentucky Reformatory after being charged with assault in 1930. It is unclear whom Carter assaulted. Apparently, two prison sentences in two separate states did nothing to change his ways. Upon his release from the Kentucky Reformatory, Carter came back to Indiana and ended up with another reformatory stay in 1936. This time he was charged with adultery and child delinquency.

Carter and the Agrue family's paths met in 1932. This is when Carter married Mary Agrue. Apparently, this marriage was a source of some of the trouble between William and Leo Agrue and Dink Carter. Carter later told police that the Agrue boys had forced him into a marriage with Mary. This is what started the grudge between the men. The marriage between Mary and Dink Carter did not last long.

The divorce between Mary and Dink Carter did not mean that the Agrue family had seen the last of Dink Carter. Carter ended up marrying their other daughter Leona in 1938. According to newspaper reports during the trial, Leona and Dink lived in a houseboat near Aurora. The spring of 1941 would see a lot of family arguments and drama between Leona's family and Carter. William's wife would later testify that at least one of the arguments stemmed from the selling of pickles. What this entailed no one really knows for sure today.

One of the more sinister accounts of the trouble between the Agrue boys and Carter was reported in the *Cincinnati Enquirer* on October 18, 1941. The article mentions that Carter had a history of sexual misconduct with women and little girls. Testimony from Bessie Agrue Breeden Wiant was the most damaging part of the trial. Mrs. Wiant claimed that Carter had been infamous for molesting girls at the Agrue farm. On the stand, Wiant told of Carter hiding in the woods with a shotgun or a rifle "pretending to hunt but actually intent only on molesting any of the girls who might go to the mailbox." He would lay in wait for one of the girls to appear, and then he would strike.

Mrs. Wiant also recalled an encounter she had with Carter in taxi. She cried and described for the court the experience of trying to fight off Carter's sexual advances once on a taxicab ride from Lawrenceburg to Dillsboro. The saddest part of the trial discussed a past history of the murdered Mary Elizabeth having had what the newspaper termed a "social disease" at the age of three after a visit to the Carter home. There are many who speculate that Carter's history of being inappropriate could have been a source of the troubles between the Agrue family and him. It was well known that two months prior to the murders, Johnston Agrue had run Carter off the property, although no one would say why. A relative of the Agrues stated that it was believed that Carter had impregnated little Mary Elizabeth, which was why Johnston Agrue had run him off the farm. It should be noted that none of the articles from the time surrounding the murders mentions this.

It is also important to note that Carter was never tried for any of the sexual allegations that were brought to light during the murder trial. The *Cincinnati Enquirer* article, however, did mention that Mary Elizabeth's murder was probably committed as a way to "silence her" about the murders of her grandparents and uncles. If the sexual allegations were true, one would also think he would have wanted to silence that getting out as well.

Interestingly, Carter's trial in October 1941 was not for all five slayings. The State of Indiana went against Carter only for the death of little Mary Elizabeth. Dearborn County prosecutor Lester Baker announced to the public that he would be seeking the electric chair. Finding jurors was a grueling task: 150 people were vetted for the trial and were dismissed for one reason or another. The Muncie, Indiana newspaper reported that jurors were "farm people, most of whom had brought their lunches." The trial officially started in Lawrenceburg on October 14, 1941.

The trial, which took place at the Dearborn County circuit courtroom, was the talk of the papers of the day. The trial was certainly the biggest and most dramatic trial of that period. It would have been the O.J. Simpson or Johnny Depp trial of its time. It seemed that each day of the trial and testimony from each witness brought about some new twist. During the trial, the first Agrue sister Carter had married testified as a witness.

That's right! Mary Agrue Breeden Carter stood up in the courtroom and declared that she and not her sister Leona was the one still married to Virginius Carter. Mary insisted that she married Carter in 1932 and testified that she had not gotten a divorce and did not think Carter had legally done so. Carter testified that he believed Mary had gone to Cincinnati to obtain the divorce and that he was free to marry her sister Leona six years later in 1938.

To add even more drama to the trial, Carter also apparently attempted to break out of the Brookville jail, where he was being held. Newspapers did not go into detail about this but only reported a statement from Sheriff Winegard that jail staff had found out that Carter had an escape plan. Of course, the drama meant that the people couldn't get enough news about it. The *Cincinnati Enquirer* reported that people lined the streets of Lawrenceburg just to catch a peek at Carter being led to the courtroom.

Unbelievably, wife Leona stood by his side throughout the trial. Despite the fact that Carter had wiped out most of her immediate family, a *Times* article reported that she had hitchhiked from her "houseboat home to visit with Carter" daily during the trial. The newspaper reported her sitting with Dink's elderly father, Tom Carter, and dabbing her eyes with a handkerchief throughout the trial.

You would be wrong if you think the trial could not get more suspenseful. During the trial, Carter claimed that the written confession he had given Sheriff Winegard was false. A *Tipton* article revealed that as Lester Baker cross-examined him and read the written confession aloud, Carter kept repeating, "I don't remember saying that." On the stand, Carter dropped an even bigger bombshell when he announced that he had not committed the murders. He blamed a man he knew by the name of Francis Graves of Switzerland County as the killer.

Carter claimed that Graves had made a confession to him when he was with him the night of May 16 in Newport, Kentucky. Of course, under examination by Prosecutor Lester Baker, he crumbled. According to a *Linton* article, when Carter was asked what he did the afternoon of the sixteenth during the killings, he told the court, "That's for me to know, and I ain't telling nobody." When this tactic didn't seem to be working, Carter then insisted that he did not kill Mrs. Agrue or the little girl; he had killed only Mr. Agrue and the two sons. He was insistent that Graves was the one who had killed the girls. Please note that Francis Graves was never arrested or brought to trial for any suspected involvement in the murders.

Carter was found guilty of the Agrue family murders on October 21, 1941. The Dearborn County court sentenced him to death and sent him to the Michigan City Prison. Carter died in the electric chair on February 10, 1942. Legend has it that the Michigan City State Prison sent a bill of fifty dollars to Dearborn County for Carter's death. Carter was sent back to Aurora for burial in the River View Cemetery. To this day, Carter is the only offender that Dearborn County, Indiana, has sentenced to die in the electric chair.

A visitor to the cemetery will see that Dink Carter was buried with his grave facing the Agrue family plot. According to the Dearborn County Historical Society, Carter was buried facing the Agrue family as a form of eternal punishment. By having his grave facing those he murdered, Carter forever faces the people he has wronged. One would think that this story is over since the victims have been laid to rest and the murderer has been caught, served his sentence and laid to rest. This is not, however, where Virginius "Dink" Carter's story ends. It is where a mysterious Dearborn County legend was born.

The legends about the glowing grave at River View Cemetery started not too long after Carter's burial. It began with people reporting seeing something glowing in the cemetery at night. Others reported that it was a grave glowing. Over the many years, it became a rite of passage to go out to the cemetery and see if you could catch a glimpse of the gravestone glowing at night.

The Agrue house and farm are no longer there. At the time the Agrues lived there, the house was known as the D.C. Wilbur place. The house used to sit at the bottom of the first hill on Laughery Creek Road. If you turn off Hussman Road onto Laughery Road, the house sat not far at all from that intersection. The house, which was not visible from the road, was unfortunately destroyed by fire in 1970. However, an owner of the house after the murders reported that the house and the land were both haunted. Even though the house is long gone, people still believe that the land is haunted. Someone living in an adjacent trailer to the property reported seeing apparitions at night. There have been reports over the years of sightings of the victims and of Carter himself. They are most often reported to walk along Laughery Creek Road at night.

3

DEARBORN COUNTY
HAUNTED RESTAURANTS

If you stop and think about it, many of life's greatest moments occur at restaurants. These locations serve as the scene of good times and sometimes bad. Going out for a nice meal is a way for many to celebrate life's achievements and sometimes sorrows such as funeral dinners or memorials. Many restaurants and bars become a part of a family's tradition to eat or to celebrate there. With so many of life's moments and celebrations at these establishments, it's no wonder these locations are sometimes thought to hold a memory and are reported to have a paranormal connection.

At least three restaurants in Dearborn County are reported to be haunted. For years, legends have been told and retold about these restaurants. This chapter discusses these locations, a little bit of history and the legends about them. Most of this section of our book comes from oral local folklore.

WHISKY'S RESTAURANT

Since opening its doors back in 1984, Whisky's Restaurant and Bar has been a Dearborn County family favorite. Located in downtown Lawrenceburg, Indiana, the restaurant is well known for its ribs, creamy potato soup and, of course, its famous peanut slaw. If you dine there, one

Above: Gabbard Park and J Miller Steakhouse & Tiffany's Saloon, located on Second Street in Aurora, Indiana.

Opposite, top: The Front Street side of Whisky's Restaurant in Lawrenceburg, Indiana. This restaurant has been a local favorite since it opened in 1984.

Opposite, bottom: Front of Whisky's Restaurant in Lawrenceburg, Indiana. Paranormal experiences have been a part of Whisky's story since the beginning.

thing is for certain: you are guaranteed to have a great meal. You may also just walk away with more than a full stomach. You may just leave with a paranormal story of your very own.

Over the years, many people who have worked at the restaurant and patrons have reportedly had paranormal experiences at the establishment since its beginning. The authors of this book are included, having both had experiences at the restaurant. The owner of Whisky's did not wish to be interviewed for this publication. However, former employees and patrons shared their experiences from over the years.

If you look up the history of the building, the county records date the building to 1865. This puts the building's establishment at the end of the Civil War. If you look at the restaurant, you can see that it was originally two houses. At some point, the houses were joined together by connecting them with a lobby area. According to local legend and folklore, the building was also once a button factory.

Indeed, according to the Indiana Historical Society, Indiana had many button factories along the Ohio and Wabash Rivers. Lawrenceburg did, in fact, have its own button factory. Although records show the location of the factory was probably at Front and Fourth Streets (where the present-day CVS sits today), no conclusive evidence suggests that the building Whisky's is in was once the factory. A post on the Dearborn County Historical

Society Facebook page recalled buttons being found when the United Community Bank was built. According to the post, a "bushel basket of these drilled shells were found, along with many whole ones collected from the Ohio River." Many in the surrounding area have found buttons when digging their property.

The building where Whisky's Restaurant is located was first constructed as two private residences. Local folklore says that in one of the homes, an older lady passed away in the room now known as "the Malt Room." It is a long-held belief that this lady's spirit has never ever left the building. The lady's presence has made herself known in several ways throughout the years.

This spirit has been known to tug at waitresses' aprons in an urgent manner. According to local message forums, one former waitress thought it was another server who needed something. When she turned to see what this person wanted, she was shocked to find that there was no one there. This event happened several times to this waitress. What is even stranger is that the tugging on the apron has also happened to others. Is it possible that it is the spirit of the lady?

The lady ghost, as she is referred to, has also been known to make her appearance through the fragrance of a strong perfume or an old type of cologne. A popular story surrounding this smell has been reported on many online forums. According to legend, one evening, there was a former manager of the restaurant who was sitting in the bar area. The restaurant had closed its doors for the night. The manager was sitting there finishing up some paperwork and just getting settled in from a busy evening of service. While sitting there, the manager started smelling a very strong perfume or cologne scent. A cold chill accompanied the smell, and the manager quickly finished up her business and got out of there for the night.

The strangest and most unsettling part of this legend is that this manager was certain that she was the only person in the building that evening. She knew beyond a shadow of a doubt that she was all alone and that all of the other employees and patrons had already gone home. This strange phenomenon has occurred frequently over the years. When the perfume smell and cold chill come around, they always emanate from the direction of the back of the room.

The lady ghost also has been known to cause patrons to feel a chill or slight breeze while sitting at their table. This is an event that the authors of this book have both experienced while dining at Whisky's. The chill is the kind of cold chill where the hair on your arms stands up. After speaking with

The rear entrance of Whisky's Restaurant, Lawrenceburg, Indiana, where a ghost is said to blow out candles at the table.

other patrons and former employees, we concluded that this event mostly occurs in the Malt Room area.

However, this strange chill has also been known to occur all over the restaurant. Along with the breeze, the candles on the tables will unexpectedly go out. When this happens, it's as if someone has gently blown the flame out. When a server is alerted, they have difficulty lighting the candles again. This is an occurrence that has been experienced by author Rebecca each time she has dinner at the establishment.

Is this the spirit of a former resident of the building? A former patron? No one knows for sure. If you decide to investigate on your own, we recommend potato soup and peanut slaw. You will not be disappointed.

THE APPLEWOOD

The Applewood Restaurant was a strong staple in Aurora, Indiana, for nineteen years. The restaurant was known for its gorgeous river views, fine dining, tasty ribs and delicious fried chicken (it was the stuff of legend for sure). One fact that any visitor to the establishment could agree on: you were guaranteed to get a great meal if you ate at the Applewood Restaurant.

People came for miles for the great food and live music acts. Visitors would come from Cincinnati just for a meal.

Sadly, Applewood closed its doors in 2013. The main reason cited for the closure was the road construction that year along Highway 56. The ongoing road construction had a horrible effect on the business. According to a 2013 article on the Eagle 99.3 website, INDOT kept moving the signs for the detour route to the restaurant.

When interviewed by Eagle 99.3, the owner of the Applewood, Donna Ruther, stated, "We just became too difficult to find for our customers from Cincinnati. Even people from Aurora told us they couldn't find how to get in here." When the Applewood Restaurant closed its doors for good, there were fifty employees who sadly lost their jobs that day.

Dearborn County records date the building to 1899, but legends say the building may be much older than that. One of the restaurant's most well-known and discussed legends comes from the turn of the nineteenth century. According to this ghostly tale, a wedding took place behind the restaurant in the area where the magnificent courtyard is today. From the river, celebratory shots rang out from nearby boats. This was something that was not unheard of during this time in history. Unfortunately, during the

Opposite: Applewood Restaurant in Aurora, Indiana, was known for its tasty ribs, delicious fried chicken and live music. It closed in 2013.

Right: Applewood Restaurant, where a heartbroken groom mourning the death of his bride is said to haunt the building.

Below: Rear courtyard of the Applewood Restaurant. Sounds of a man crying have been reported from the attic area of the building.

View of the Ohio River from the rear of the Applewood property in Aurora, Indiana.

ceremony, the bride was struck and killed immediately by one of the stray bullets from the shotguns on the nearby boats.

The bride died in her groom's arms. The heartbroken groom could not bear the death of his bride. Stricken by grief, and in complete terror and shock, the groom entered the Applewood Restaurant building, and according to local folklore, he hanged himself in the attic. From that day forward, the spirit of the groom has been said to make his presence in the building known.

Over the years that the building held various establishments, former patrons and employees have had many experiences. The most common strange phenomenon involves the sounds of footsteps from the attic or upstairs area as if someone is walking around. This has occurred when it is known there is no one else above. Chills and sounds of a man crying have all been reported from the attic area of the building. The building is empty and is currently listed for sale as of the time of this publication.

THE DOVER TAVERN

Driving down State Route 1, you will notice a large, two-story, red brick building that has stood at the intersection of North Dearborn Road and State Route 1 for as long as anyone around the county can remember. It is a large structure with a long porch that faces North Dearborn Road. The building and land that it sits on have an interesting history. It originally served as a stagecoach rest stop and tavern. Over the many years that it has stood, the building has always housed some sort of bar or a restaurant. Most refer to this building as the Dover Tavern. Many do not realize that this building also has a Civil War history.

In July 1863, General John Hunt Morgan and 2,500 of his troops marched through Dearborn County. In fact, according to the historical marker at North Dearborn Road and State Route 1, Morgan and his men did, in fact, raid and loot the two taverns that were located in Dover during that time. The building next door to the Dover Tavern was also a tavern and dance hall during this time.

The dance hall in the building next door was located on the second floor. According to a historical marker located across the street, that building

General John Hunt Morgan historical marker at the corner of North Dearborn Road and Route 1, located in Guilford, Indiana.

General John Hunt Morgan trail marker at the intersection of North Dearborn Road and Route 1, located in Guilford, Indiana.

had an upstairs dance hall that could be reached by using a hand-operated elevator. The building operated as a bed-and-breakfast for several years. It is now a private residence.

In her 1995 book, *Thunderbolt: Revisit Southeastern Indiana with John Hunt Morgan,* author Lora Cahill shares that when Morgan and his raiders marched through Dover, they raided both of the taverns. At that time, a man named James Murtaugh owned the dance hall next door to the Dover Tavern. Murtaugh tried in vain to stop Morgan from raiding his tavern. It was no use. "The more he protested, the more damage they did." They marched out of town with their loot from both taverns, heading up North Dearborn Road.

Morgan and his men ended up intercepting a funeral procession occurring down North Dearborn Road. The funeral was for a twelve-year-old boy named William Glardon Jr., who, according to local stories, passed from a ruptured appendix. According Cahill's book, undertakers in that period always had the best-looking horses.

Morgan's men ended up taking the two horses that were leading the hearse carriage with the coffin. However, he did not allow the horses of the people attending the funeral procession to be stolen. In *Thunderbolt*, Morgan is quoted as saying, "Where I come from down south, we respect the dead." It is interesting to note, though, that Morgan did replace those horses with ones that they had so that the funeral could go on.

In recent years, the Dover Tavern has housed many different establishments. In the past twenty years, it has been a sports bar, a pizza place and, most recently, a barbecue restaurant.

Former patrons and employees of the establishments that have occupied the Dover Tavern have reported ghostly phenomena occurring in the building over the years. One former patron says that he remembers it always being cold in the building. He recalled that "no matter the time of year, there would be a cold chill that would go past you." This would occur even in the hot summer.

On the second floor of the building is an apartment. However, it has been reported over the years that the apartment could not be rented. Tenants would complain of hearing men talking. Sometimes it sounded as if the talking was coming from the tavern below. The talking would

Dover Tavern in Guilford, Indiana, at the intersection of North Dearborn Road and Route 1, where complaints of ghostly voices have been reported.

be accompanied by the sound of some heavy footsteps—footsteps that sounded as if someone wearing old-fashioned boots was downstairs walking around.

Other times, the sounds of men talking seemed to be coming from outside of the building. Whenever someone looked to see who was there, every time there would be no one around. This would happen even after the building was closed up for the evening.

The Dover Tavern building is currently sitting vacant. The last business to occupy the space was Stouts Brickhouse, and it was a delicious barbecue restaurant. The restaurant closed its doors in 2018. It may be under renovation from the looks of things and the dumpster outside at the time of this writing. One must wonder if there will continue to be ghost stories from the building in the future.

4

HAUNTED SCHOOLS
OF DEARBORN COUNTY

MOORES HILL CARNEGIE HALL

One of the most recognizable and historical buildings in all of Dearborn County would have to be the Carnegie Hall located in Moores Hill, Indiana. It was initially built for Moores Hill College. For over seventy-nine years, Carnegie Hall provided education to the citizens of Dearborn County. Originally, Carnegie Hall offered students the opportunity to gain baccalaureate and master's degrees, and later, as a public school, it housed students in the first through twelfth grades. This is one building that has truly stood the test of time. Today, there is much lore and mystery surrounding the building.

It all started in 1854. This is when John C. Moore (son of Adam Moore, founder of Moores Hill) and Morton Justis donated the land for the Moores Hill Male and Female Collegiate Institute. The location of the college was an excellent choice. According to an 1859 advertisement, it was located right along the Ohio and Mississippi Railroad line. Moores Hill is also only forty miles southwest of Cincinnati. Student tuition was anywhere from eighteen to thirty-two dollars. There were extra charges if a student wished to take painting, French, German or a drawing class. According to the Indiana Historical Society, a woman named Jane Church has the honor of being the first graduate of Moores Hill College. She graduated in 1858 with a "Mistress of English Literature" degree.

Moores Hill Sign at Highway 350 and Main Street. Moores Hill is the location of two haunted schools in the area.

The legendary Carnegie Hall, built in 1907, unique for its blond brick. Red brick was associated with most Carnegie buildings of the time.

The first building for the college was constructed in 1856. It was a massive, eighty-by-eighty-foot, three-story, red brick structure that was named Moore Hall after John C. Moore. The college grew around Moore Hall to include several different outbuildings. Several still stand to this day and are now private residences.

In 1887, the college officially changed its name to Moores Hill College. At this time, the college was the sixth coeducational college in the entire United States. Moores Hill College was growing fast. A dormitory was built in 1895. It began to offer athletics. A gymnasium was later constructed in 1896. With the growth of the college, it soon became obvious that the institution needed more room. Soon, the dream of building what we now know as Carnegie Hall began.

In the early part of the twentieth century, a businessman and philanthropist named Andrew Carnegie was becoming renowned for funding many libraries and public buildings all over the United States. He was personally responsible for the building of over 2,500 such edifices across the world, and Moores Hill's Carnegie Hall was one of them. Andrew Carnegie pledged to give half of the $36,000 in construction costs, and therefore the building was named after him.

The cornerstone was laid for Carnegie Hall in 1907. The building was completed in 1908. Interestingly, the building is not the classic red brick associated with many of the Andrew Carnegie buildings of the time. The people of Moores Hill wanted the building to be unique. Blond brick was used instead, to set it apart from the rest.

In 1915, a fire destroyed Moore Hall. The building was a total loss, and it forever changed Moores Hill College. After the fire, the fate of the college was unknown. After some consideration, the college resumed classes in the newer Carnegie Hall and held classes there for two years until the college relocated to Evansville, Indiana, in 1917. It was renamed Evansville College and remains there to this day.

In 1918, the building was given to the Town of Moores Hill for use as a public school. It operated as an elementary and high school. In the 1960s, Moores Hill School consolidated with Dillsboro, Aurora and Manchester schools to form the South Dearborn Community School Corporation. The last high school class graduated in 1978 when South Dearborn High School opened its doors. In the fall of '78, Moores Hill students went to the new high school in Aurora. The elementary and junior high school remained in Carnegie Hall until 1987, when Moores Hill Elementary School was opened.

Main doors at Carnegie Hall, original location of Moores Hill College, which later became Evansville College when it relocated to Evansville, Indiana, in 1917.

Left: Hitching post for horses on the corner of Carnegie Hall, Moores Hill, Indiana.

Right: Carnegie Hall steps showing the wear of decades of foot traffic. This building provided education to Dearborn County for over seventy-nine years.

Over the years, there have been many legends associated with Carnegie Hall. One of the most mysterious occurrences that happens is security alarms that seem to set themselves off. Moores Hill town marshals and the Dearborn County Sheriff's Department have responded many times for interior alarms being set off from inside the building. Upon closer investigation, the officer who responds sees that the doors are secure and that no one is around. Most officers in the area hate being called out to the alarms at Carnegie Hall. It is a scenario that has played out time and again.

One of the most popular legends is about a mule and a farmer who are often seen on the third floor. Just as soon as the duo is seen, the apparition disappears. This ghost story may actually be related to a real incident.

According to one of Carnegie Hall's caretakers, a group of high school boys in the 1920s or '30s decided to play a prank. They thought it would be funny to bring a mule into the building. The only thing the boys did not realize was that mules do not go down steps naturally. Animals such as cows, horses and mules cannot see their feet well and are hesitant to go down steps unless trained. The students got the mule up; however, the stubborn animal just would not budge to go back down.

Above: Carnegie Hall Auditorium, where many graduations, concerts and other local events have happened over the years.

Opposite, top: Carnegie Hall auditorium balcony. Some paranormal activities associated with the building are thought to be residual hauntings.

Opposite, bottom: The third floor of Carnegie Hall with the class of 1975 graffiti, where the ghost of a farmer and mule is seen.

How did they get the mule down? Legend says that they had to use rope and take the mule out of an upstairs window instead. Perhaps people are seeing what is referred to as a residual haunting—a replay of the mule being on the third floor of Carnegie Hall. The animal was not harmed or killed getting it down from the third floor.

The identity of the farmer is unknown. According to local schoolchildren, a farmer once hanged himself in the bell tower of Carnegie Hall. When asked, the staff would not confirm this. The only thing known for sure is that there is one official death recorded at Carnegie, and it is of an unknown nature. Is there any truth to the legend of the farmer and his death? As the caretaker pointed out, the area was home to nothing but farmers and is still largely an agricultural community. The identity of this spirit and his story seem to have been lost over the years.

MOORES HILL ELEMENTARY SCHOOL

The year 1987 was such an exciting one for the town of Moores Hill, Indiana. The new elementary school was opened that year, and the first students started classes. Carnegie Hall had served the town well as a school, but it was now time for a new educational building. The "new" building sat adjacent to the spot where Moore Hall had once stood proudly. An old gymnasium used by Carnegie was reused and fit into the construction of the

Moores Hill Elementary School in Moores Hill, Indiana, opened its doors in 1987 and provided education to students for thirty-four years.

building. Some reports say that the gym was from the 1930s, and it replaced an older structure from the late 1800s. Plans were made to incorporate this gym into the elementary structure.

One former student who reminisced on how exciting the opening of the building was had this to say: "We moved over to the new building in the middle of my fifth-grade year. Everything was new," he remarked. "All of the desks, the chairs, you could smell the new, fresh paint." It certainly seems like it was an exciting time.

For over thirty-four years, the building served the community well and educated many students from kindergarten through the eighth grade. The school even had a preschool there at one time. Over the last few years that the school was open, the district faced declining enrollment. In 2015, Lawrenceburg local radio station Eagle 99.3 reported that the enrollment in 2008–9 was 3,122 students. However, in 2015 the enrollment dropped to just 2,656 students. In 2015, rumors began that the district was going to make the tough decision to close Moores Hill Elementary School.

For the next six years, the school district monitored enrollment, which continued to make a sharp decline. According to a *Dearborn County Register*

Moores Hill Elementary School is the site of several hauntings that are often attributed to former students and staff.

The Moores Hill Elementary School sign. Sadly, the school closed after the 2020–21 school year due to declining enrollment.

article from February 23, 2021, the South Dearborn Community School board voted 7–0 to close Moores Hill Elementary School at the end of the 2020–21 school year, ending an era.

With the closing of the school came the end of the ghost stories that many staff and students had experienced and reported over the many years. The most familiar and strange occurrence associated with the building is the sighting of the little blonde girl. She is always seen and heard skipping throughout the building. She is thought to be the spirit of a student who was murdered shortly after moving from Moores Hill. Many people believe that her spirit remains because that is the last place she was happy.

One evening, a teacher who was working late grading papers heard the sound of a child skipping and singing down the hallway. She looked out the window of her classroom door just in time to see a glimpse of a blonde little girl walking past her classroom. The teacher rose from her desk to confront the child, knowing it was long past hours that students should have been in the building. When she got to the hallway, there was no one there and no place for the child to have disappeared to.

Another strange phenomenon that staff reported is the sound of lockers slamming from the area of the old junior high. There have also been reports of a man's voice being heard in the gym, but no one can tell what is being said. Sounds of basketballs being bounced on the gym floor echo when no one is there. Some have heard the sound of an old weight-lifting bench that has not been used in many years. Many students reported hearing footsteps in the main bathroom in front of the library when they were the only student in the restroom area.

Author Rebecca has her own story associated with the library lights:

I worked at Moores Hill Elementary as a library aide. I always propped open the library closet to make it easier to get laptop computers, cords or other items needed during class. Often, I would leave the light in the closet on. One day while sitting at my desk in between classes, I noticed that the library closet light kept going off on me. It was as if someone was flipping the switch off. It happened several times when I was the only person in the library—never when a class or another teacher was with me.

The stones outside of Moores Hill Elementary School. The big, round stone is from the Moores Hill Mill.

At first, I was convinced that it had to be a bad switch. Being new to the school, I had no idea about the ghost lore associated with the building. So I turned in a maintenance ticket for the closet light. The school's electrician came out and changed the light switch in the closet, telling me there was nothing wrong with it. The light did not shut off while he was there. As soon as he left the building and I went back over to my desk, the light once again shut off. I never propped open the closet door again.

A similar experience occurred involving the small round ceiling lights running around the library's center. These lights are on a round dimmer switch that makes an audible click when turned off. Once again, I was waiting alone for the next class when the lights turned off. Again, I was not thinking of ghosts, so I turned in a ticket for these lights. The maintenance man came out to investigate, and once again, there was nothing wrong upon closer investigation.

The lights did not do this while he was there. Just like the time before, as soon as he left and I was alone in the library, the lights did it again. This time, I heard the unmistakable click of the switch being turned off. I never used those lights again for the remainder of my time there.

Who is responsible for the lights in the library? No one knows for sure. Staff who I have shared this with and I have a suspicion that it may be the spirit of a former maintenance man, Tom, who was known for playing pranks. Tom had played a prank shutting the hallway light off on me in another building I had worked in while he was still alive. The building is not currently in use since the end of the 2020–21 school year. It will be interesting to see if there are any further ghost sightings in the future.

St. John Lutheran School

In the 1850s, German Lutherans living in Aurora, Indiana, needed a place to worship and a school for the education of their children. These early inhabitants first began a Lutheran school on the banks of the Ohio River near Third Street, and they conducted their worship in a building purchased from the Baptists in Aurora on Broadway Street. According to a March 4, 2010 article in the *Dearborn County Register*, the congregation "had expanded that church once by adding a balcony, the congregation decided to build a new church, the one it inhabits today." St. Johns School is the oldest school system in Aurora, predating the public school system.

St. John Lutheran Church and School in Aurora, Indiana, is the oldest school in the county and predates the public school system.

Eventually, the congregation wanted a more permanent structure and for both the church and school building to be together. In 1874, the brick structure that we know today was built. The building has the ability to seat 260 people for service, and its most notable feature is the 105-foot steeple that can be seen from all over the area, especially from the State Road 350 hill as you approach US 50.

Church worship and education were extremely important to the congregation. They built the first of three Lutheran school buildings on Mechanic Street in 1882. A second two-story structure was built in 1901, and the last and current building was built in 1957. This building is adjacent to the church at the corner of Third and Mechanic Streets and is still in use today.

St. John Lutheran School is the last and only Lutheran school in the entire area. It continues to offer a Christian education to students in preschool through the eighth grade.

It is also rumored to be haunted.

One strange phenomenon that has been reported is the sound of people in the hallways when no one is there. Several staff members have reported

St. John Lutheran School, Third Street entrance. Ghostly footsteps are heard on the staircase landing of the Third Street doors.

hearing footsteps. These footsteps are always heard on the staircase landing of the Third Street doors. There is also talking that is heard when no one is around.

A former custodian reported once hearing the sound of a baby crying. He investigated to see what was going on and, upon investigating, never found the source of the sound. He was working late and alone in the building. He said that it was as if the baby was moving around, and the sound would change where it was coming from as he was walking around.

This same employee also experienced hearing noises coming from the school office late one night. "It sounded as if someone was in the principal's office shuffling papers around," he said. "Eventually, I learned to just put my headphones in while cleaning and ignore anything I heard around me."

Another employee shared an experience she had involving her son and granddaughter. While she was working late one evening, her son and granddaughter were playing hide and seek in the school while they waited on her. The granddaughter was hiding in the science lab. When her father found her, she said to him, "Find that girl now, Daddy," and pointed to the corner of the room. There was nothing there.

NORTH DEARBORN ELEMENTARY SCHOOL

The growth of communities in North Dearborn County in the 1950s meant the area was going to need a bigger high school. There were three smaller schools—Guilford, West Harrison and Bright High Schools—that made the decision to consolidate and form North Dearborn High School. Those schools then became elementary schools. The site of the building of this new school was farmland that a man named Roy Lutz sold to the school.

Construction began in the late '50s, and for the 1959 school year, North Dearborn High School opened its doors to students. The facilities were like nothing the area had seen before. For fourteen years, the school served the community well as a high school.

The high school was well known for providing a high level of education. It was one of the only schools in the area that taught Latin. The school had an impressive history in sports, winning four basketball sectional titles in its fourteen years. It was also the alma mater of New York Yankees and Chicago White Sox outfielder Jim Lyttle, who graduated from North Dearborn in the early 1960s. The high school band, under Charlie Green's direction, was considered one of the best in the area during this time. The fudge that the band sold as a fundraiser is legendary.

North Dearborn Elementary School in Guilford, Indiana, where a teacher saw the ghostly apparition of her long-lost brother.

In 1973, the State of Indiana was pushing for schools to consolidate. There was a push for smaller schools that held a lower enrollment to come together and join their resources. This is how the Sunman Dearborn Community School corporation was formed in 1968. The decision was made in the early 1970s that both Sunman High School and North Dearborn would combine. Both of these schools were closed in 1973 to form East Central High School.

At that time, North Dearborn was converted to an elementary school. For the next forty-two years, the building served students in grades kindergarten through fourth grade. The decision was made by the school corporation to close the building at the end of the 2015 school year. The building was demolished in December 2021, taking with it lots of memories and, according to what some say, ghosts.

One well-known ghost story involves a teacher who was all alone working in her classroom late one night. The teacher was hard at work when out of the corner of her eye she noticed that there was someone sitting at her desk with their feet propped up on it. She looked closer and noticed it was an apparition of her brother sitting there. She recognized him, his overalls and work boots. She couldn't believe her eyes or what she was seeing because her

The Sawdon Ridge and North Dearborn Road sign is all that remains of the old North Dearborn Elementary School.

brother had been killed in an accident a short time beforehand. Her brother had a connection to the building, having worked on the construction of the addition. As soon as her eyes met his, he smiled at her and then quickly disappeared. The teacher was not sure how to explain what exactly she had seen. She did not see her brother again after that, but she did not ever feel alone in the building after that day.

This is not the only strange occurrence in the building.

For years, there were stories and rumors of what could be referred to as classic haunting behavior. Staff and students reported feeling cold spots and feelings of being watched while alone in the building. One of the most common phenomena reported over the years was the sound of children running in the hallways.

The sound of the footsteps running was something that was especially heard on the second floor and from below. People complained of hearing the sounds of footsteps in the hallway on the second floor when no one else was there. One time a group of teachers all heard it while working in the building. One teacher went up to confront whoever it was, only to get to the stairwell landing and realize that there was no one upstairs.

Often, people in the building would hear the sounds of whispering and low talking but could not quite make out what was being said. Staff working alone in the evenings reported that they would hear the sounds of what seemed to be doors slamming when they were certain that there was no one else around.

The building was razed in 2021. It will be interesting in the future to see what becomes of the land and property. Will the ghosts reside in whatever is built there? Only time will tell.

5

ST. MARY'S CHURCH RECTORY

When driving through Aurora, one can't help but notice all the beautiful churches lining the streets. There are twelve official churches that call Aurora home, but none are quite as beautiful as the historical buildings that can be found downtown. One such example can be seen on the corner of Fourth and Judiciary Streets with St. Mary of the Immaculate Conception Catholic Church, or "St. Mary's," as the locals refer to it. Its beautiful brick exterior, striking steeple and ornate stained-glass windows are hard to miss. This building and the people it serves have been part of Aurora's history for over 150 years.

The first Catholic church to be founded in the area was St. Lawrence in Lawrenceburg in 1842, but as the population increased, the need for more congregations in the area grew. Dearborn County was growing fast due to German and Irish immigrants migrating to the area in search of work. St. Mary's started in the late 1840s when a local Catholic, Mr. O'Brien, invited Father Bishop Purcell from nearby Cincinnati to read mass in his home. In the early days of the church, members of the congregation met at various homes in Aurora, the town hall or the schoolhouse. The first church building was built in 1855 by Father Koch and became known as the "little church on the hill." St. Mary's was not officially founded as a parish by the archdiocese until 1857.

The school itself had been operating for as long as the church when early settlers pushed for a way to provide a Catholic education to their children. Finding a teacher was not easy, and children were educated at St. Lawrence

St. Mary's Church in Aurora, Indiana, was originally founded in 1857. The current building was built in 1864.

for many years. A school was formed in 1855, with the church building doubling as the school. Early students were taught in both English and German. This was one of the first schools formed in the area, second only to St. John's Lutheran School, which was founded in 1850. The first teachers, Mr. Baker and Mr. Kline, were hired by early parishioners.

Dearborn County was booming in the 1850s due to increases in industry in the area. Over time, the need for a larger building became inevitable. In 1863, Father Klein, who was the first resident priest, bought the lots the church stands on today. He advanced $1,500 for the purchase of the land, and construction of the new building began shortly after. Father Klein acted as architect and superintendent for the project. Because so many members of the congratulation were employed in the trades, these parishioners completed some of the construction themselves. In the book *History of Dearborn and Ohio Counties, Indiana*, published in 1885, it is mentioned that "the membership being poor, after performing their daily labor, would gather in after supper and place the stone and brick upon the ground and scaffold for the masons to work upon during the day, thereby dispensing with the usual attendant." Workers were even able to reuse salvaged bricks from the original church to construct a school building in 1866. Construction of the main church building was completed in 1864, with the steeple being completed a decade later in 1876. The church and school ran faithfully until the 1940s, when the need came to update the buildings.

The parish began to raise money for a new school building, but then the pastor, Father Dennis Spaulding, saw the need for a rectory to be built to house pastors and visiting members of the archdiocese. The original rectory was built in the 1920s, but it was too small for the demands of the time. The parish shifted goals, and a new rectory was finished in the 1950s. The church did manage to get its school building in 1959 after a generous gift from a parishioner, John Kirby. Kirby left his home on Fifth Street to the church as well to serve as a home for the sisters.

The school was then staffed by nuns from the Sisters of Providence from St. Mary of the Woods from 1866 to 1880 and then by the Sisters of St. Francis of Oldenburg from 1880 to 1996, when the last sister retired. The school served as a high school from 1913 to 1937. However, the high school was closed in 1937 due to a lack of teachers.

The church and school continued to grow, celebrating milestone after milestone. A parish center was built in 1982. The center houses a gymnasium, a kitchen, locker rooms, classrooms, a meeting room and storage areas. The building was mostly used by the school at the time, but it was also used to host

The Parsonage of St. Mary's Church & School was built in the 1950s to house pastors and visiting members of the archdiocese.

large parish gatherings. The school continued to provide quality education for a little over one hundred students in kindergarten through eighth grade until it closed its doors in 2022.

Outside of education, St. Mary's Parish hosts the St. Vincent de Paul Food Pantry, providing nourishment and assistance to those in need. The organization also provides religious education, help with finding employment, youth programs and many other initiatives. According to the parish website, membership at St. Mary's is about four hundred households, which makes it the largest parish territory in the archdiocese of Indianapolis.

One may wonder how this beloved parish belongs in a book about hauntings, but locals are familiar with the ghostly tales that surround St. Mary's. Oddly, the ghost stories do not involve the church itself but rather the rectory. This is not surprising considering the long history of priests and guests that have lived within these walls over the years. The legend is so well known that the church is one of the many spots on the Aurora Ghost Walk hosted each fall around Halloween. The rectory stopped being used as a home for pastors in 1993 and now serves as the parish offices.

The most common complaints of ghostly activity come in the form of noises. It is not uncommon to hear footsteps, disembodied voices or the sounds of doors closing from afar. Cold spots can be felt throughout the building. Many visitors to the rectory claim to feel as though they are being watched or like someone is staring at them. Others say they felt like they were being touched and felt the hair on their arms stand up when moving to certain areas of the building.

One local resident, who wishes to remain anonymous, encountered what they believed to be a priest walking across the room late one evening. They were cleaning the rectory on behalf of the church when out of the corner of their eye, they could see the dark figure of a man walk across the room. The figure was outlined with the shape of a robe similar to what would have been worn during mass. When they turned to confront the figure, it disappeared. Startled by the experience, they packed up their cleaning supplies and left the building.

Another complaint is that whatever is haunting the rectory likes to play pranks on those in the building. Volunteers and members of the church have reported odd happenings like items going missing or being moved with no

The parsonage of St. Mary's Church & School. The ghost of the former priest is said to roam the building.

explanation. One volunteer had their set of keys go missing off a desk and show up two hours later on the kitchen counter. They had never gone into the kitchen before that moment.

The ghost, or ghosts, haunting the rectory are said not to feel malicious. All those who have experienced the activity say that it feels as though it is more curious or playful than anything else. Most assume that the hauntings must come from a former priest who once served at the parish. No one will ever know for sure.

6

HAUNTED PRIVATE RESIDENCES

SUTTON MEDICAL OFFICE

In 1836, Dr. George Sutton began what would become a long medical practice in Aurora, Indiana. His career would span the next fifty years. Aurora was a newer city at that time, having been established only seventeen years prior in 1819. The town was in desperate need of a doctor, and luckily for them, Dr. Sutton arrived that spring. In two years' time, Sutton's medical practice had grown and become quite successful.

Dr. George Sutton was born on June 10, 1812, in London, England. He, along with his family, came to the United States in 1819 when he was seven years old. He obtained his medical training in Ohio, and by 1836, he was looking for somewhere to settle down and begin practicing medicine.

Dr. Sutton has most commonly been referred to by many as a pioneer doctor, but he was most definitely much more than that. Sutton is famous for his writings and studies trying to end the various epidemics and illnesses that were affecting Indiana during this time. Sutton served as the president of the Indiana State Medical Society. He also served the City of Aurora as its seventh mayor from 1863 to 1867.

Dr. George Sutton and his family built a remarkable home atop the hill above Mechanic Street, overlooking the town, in 1850. This house was razed in 1937, and Sutton's grandson built a new home there in 1939. The new house still stands there today. The hill has been named after him and is

HAUNTED DEARBORN COUNTY, INDIANA

Dr. George Sutton's medical office building at 315 Third Street in Aurora, Indiana. It is now a private residence.

called Sutton's Hill. Every Christmas, the family puts a large star on top of the house, which can be seen from downtown Aurora. The star was built in 1939 by Dr. Sutton's grandson George and his wife, Mary. This star is still displayed today, and it is part of Aurora's tradition to see the Sutton Star.

One of the illnesses that Dr. Sutton fought so tirelessly to end was cholera. Cholera had popped up in and around the Ohio River Valley in the 1830s. Upon Dr. Sutton's arrival to the town, he heard and wrote about the stories in the area. Dearborn County faced an outbreak in 1833. The doctor wrote extensively about the illness.

Apparently, in May 1833, a steamship stopped on the Ohio River near Tanners Creek to bury one of the crew members who had passed from cholera. Unfortunately, the illness spread to one of the men who helped bury the crewmate, a man named Page Cheek. According to Dr. Sutton's writings, Cheek seemed normal the next day, even plowing a cornfield near Wilson Creek. Illness struck him in the middle of the night, however, and he passed within a few short hours. People who attended Cheek's funeral also came down with cholera. It spread around the Aurora area quickly. According to Dr. Sutton, "It is impossible now to ascertain the number of deaths which occurred, as no account of this epidemic in Dearborn County was ever published." Records were not well kept, so we will likely never know how many succumbed to cholera.

In 1849, another cholera outbreak hit Indiana hard. It was first noticed in Indianapolis and its surrounding area. This illness spread quickly because of the railroad, and it was thought that the steamships that traveled along the Ohio River were also another way that the illness was spread. According to the Indiana Academy of Science, the second-worst case of cholera in Indiana that year occurred in Aurora.

On May 1, 1849, citizens of Aurora began experiencing an illness that caused extreme diarrhea and vomiting. This is, of course, a hallmark sign of cholera. Four people had died by May 13. According to former Purdue University professor and author Donald E. Bloodgood in his 1951 book *Early Health Conditions in Indiana*, the city of Aurora responded by lighting large fires "at the corners of the streets, and cannons were fired every twenty-five minutes for four or five hours." By the following day, the number of dead from cholera had risen to fourteen in Aurora.

Unfortunately, this was a personal illness for the doctor, as the Sutton family all caught the sickness this time. The doctor and his wife lost their youngest son to the epidemic in 1849. In a report that he made before the state medical society in 1885, Sutton recalled that of all the various illnesses he had seen in fifty years of practicing medicine in Aurora, cholera was the worst. By August 27, 1849, 132 people in Aurora had died from the cholera outbreak.

A November 8, 2019 *Main Street Aurora* Facebook post quoted Dr. Sutton's report before the Indiana State Medical Board. In the report, Sutton told the board about the cholera epidemic: "After only a few hours' illness, and my youngest child sank to what appeared the lowest stage of collapse from which a patient could recover." Dr. Sutton felt that he knew what was causing the illness to spread, and he thought he knew what needed to happen to end this suffering. Dr. Sutton felt that sanitation played a part in the spread of cholera and that getting a handle on that was needed to help prevent the pandemic from spreading.

In 1870, Dr. Sutton had the building that is located at 315 Third Street built. This replaced a previous building that had been his office. For the next sixteen years, 315 Third Street would serve as his medical office. It is a two-story brick building on a limestone foundation, and it has what is known as a mansard roof. The mansard roof is a unique design element that allows for the attic space to be a useful area of a building.

Dr. Sutton and his sons all practiced medicine out of this building. Dr. George Sutton passed away in 1886. His sons continued to practice and use the building as a medical office until 1921, according to the National Register of Historic Places form that was filed in 1994. At some time during the 1930s, the building changed from a medical office and was converted and used as apartments until 1992.

According to the Discover Indiana website, the house was used as a medical office once again after 1992 by Dr. Sutton's great-grandson. The building has been on the National Register of Historic places since 1994. It appears that the building remained in the Sutton family until sometime in the early 2000s, when it changed hands into private ownership. It remains privately owned to this day.

The building is mentioned if you take the walking ghost tour that Main Street Aurora has every October. Some of the stories that are told about the home concern reports of hearing someone coughing loudly from upstairs. It sounds as if there is a man coughing, and whenever someone goes to check, there is no one else around. This occurrence has happened many times to various people who have been in the building over the years.

Cold spots and the sounds of footsteps around the building are also reported. A former resident told of hearing what sounded like a man talking from the rear of the building. After they went to check this out, there was no one there.

Who is it that is being heard in the building? Is it possibly the spirit of Dr. Sutton or perhaps one of his former patients? We may never know for sure.

GAFF DRY GOODS, MERCANTILE STORE AND APARTMENT

An impressive two-story brick apartment building sits at 201 Second Street. For at least 179 years, this building has stood at the corner of Judiciary and Second Streets. Many pass this well-kept building each day. Yet visitors to the town do not realize that this building is connected to the history of Aurora and one of its founding fathers. It is also rumored to be haunted.

You see, the downstairs of this building is where Thomas Gaff and his brothers ran their dry goods and mercantile store. The Gaffs came to Aurora

Right: 201 Second Street. The Gaff family lived here before building Hillforest. Thomas Gaff operated a dry goods store on the bottom floor.

Below: Back view of Gaff apartment and dry goods store. Caroline Gaff died from scarlet fever in the second-floor apartment in 1853.

in 1843 after the 1937 panic had made operating their distillery business and store in Pennsylvania difficult. They came to Aurora to try their hand at a business in a new area. Aurora was getting well-known and established during this period. The city was only twenty-four years old, in terms of being an official city, at the time the Gaffs came to town.

It was also this building where the Gaffs would live upstairs, above the dry goods and mercantile store. The household included Thomas and Sarah Gaff; their children; Thomas's mother, Margaret; and his unmarried sisters. This meant cramped and close quarters. They would live in this apartment while Hillforest was being built and would move into Hillforest in 1855.

Official county records of old structures in Dearborn County are sometimes hard to trace. The reason for this is all of the floodings that have occurred. The original courthouse also burned at one point, and many early land and property records were lost. People were instructed to go with their copy of the deed to have it recorded, and most people did that. However, not everyone did.

On November 7, 1853, Thomas and Sarah Gaff's fifteen-year-old daughter passed away from the effects of what her obituary referred to as lung fever in this upstairs apartment. Lung fever is what we know today as pneumonia. When Hillforest Mansion staff were asked about Caroline Gaff's death, they reported that scarlet fever took the young lady's life. Both of these illnesses were rampant at the time of Caroline's passing. Both were common illnesses that were affecting Aurora residents. She was just three days short of her sixteenth birthday. Although Thomas was one of the people responsible for incorporating River View Cemetery, Caroline is not buried there. She was laid to rest in Cincinnati in Spring Grove Cemetery. One has to wonder if Dr. George Sutton treated Caroline.

Today, the building is used as apartments. According to current residents of the apartments, the sounds of someone lightly walking up and down the stairs can be heard during the night. The sound is as if there is a lady walking the steps and wearing old-style shoes, the kind that clack on the floor when you walk. What is even stranger is that Hillforest Mansion experienced haunting when Caroline's portrait was returned to the mansion.

Speculation is that it may be Caroline's spirit who is walking the steps at the apartment building during the night. Is Caroline's spirit not at rest and looking for her family?

French/Kirsch/Neaman House

A stately red two-story brick building stands at 506 Second Street, next to the old railroad depot. For well over 150 years, this building has been a witness to the good times and bad in the small river town, yet many do not realize the neat history that these walls hold or the mystery and intrigue surrounding the building and its inhabitants.

The legends begin in August 1875, when Jacob and Barbara Kirsch purchased the building from James and Ellen French. At the time, the building had been operating as a saloon and a boardinghouse since its construction in 1870. It was known at that time as the "French house." Jacob and Barbara would rename the business the Kirsch House upon purchasing it. It went by that name and was also known as the Kirsch Hotel and Pub.

An 1876 advertisement lauded the establishment as "the most desirable place in the city of Aurora at which to stop. Good wines, liquors, and cigars." The business could not have been situated in a better location. Being right next to the train depot meant that travelers to the town of Aurora would see the restaurant. It was also only a few blocks from where the riverboats would dock. The proximity meant that those needing to rent a room would also be able to do that.

The Kirsch House on Second Street in Aurora, Indiana. This building has been a witness to Dearborn County history for over 152 years.

Backside of Kirsch House. Site of the suicide of Joseph Smithfield Wymond on July 3, 1910.

There are a few legends that are associated with the house and the people who lived there. In 1887, Jacob Kirsch was part of a lynching that occurred in Aurora during the Aurora Fair. The man who was lynched was a bricklayer named William Watkins who had come to Aurora to work on one of the businesses on Second Street. Apparently, Watkins had been drinking. When Watkins's employer, Louis Hilbert, asked him to get back to work, he was stabbed by Watkins.

Although there were two Aurora policemen present when this occurred, a mob ensued. Before Watkins could be taken into the Aurora Jail, men in the town gathered up and took Watkins from the policemen. The group, including Jacob Kirsch, was outraged and took a rope and dragged Watkins to the property of the Aurora Distillery (located on what is now called Importing Street). This is where they hanged Watkins from scaffolding over an old well on the property.

Jacob Kirsch and the other men who were involved with the lynching—William Gerlach, George Langford, Julius Hauck, Charles Baker, Joseph Schwartz, Adolph Schultz, William Thompson, Cyrus Sterling, Albert Bruce and Valentine Grossman—were sued by Watkins's widow. Eliza Watkins sued the men for $10,000 in damages, claiming the men had taken support for herself and their three children, as Watkins had been the sole provider for the family.

According to court documents, some kind of agreement was reached between all parties and Eliza Watkins, although it is not recorded what that arrangement was. In February 1887, Jacob sold the home to his wife, Barbara. This was something that was rare for the period, as most women did not own their own land. Barbara would remain the owner of the home until 1921, when she sold it.

There is one known death and one funeral that we know took place out of the residence. On July 3, 1910, Joseph Smithfield Wymond, the Kirschs' son-in-law, died by suicide at the residence. Wymond was married to Kirsch's daughter Carrie. According to the family, Wymond shot himself in the rear of the residence. Wymond's funeral is also said to have taken place out of the residence.

Why did Wymond shoot himself? He was going insane from the effects of syphilis. The illness was too great for him to bear. Today there are reports

Blue Lick Well in Aurora, Indiana. Discovered in 1888 by Kirsch's son-in-law, CB Lore. Legend says it was a healing well.

of people feeling uneasy in the rear of the house. Many also have the feeling that they are being watched or the hair on their arms stands up when they walk past the rear of the residence. This has been experienced by those who are unaware of the suicide that occurred there.

The Blue Lick Mineral Well in Aurora also has a connection to the Kirsch family. The well is located at the corner of Highway 50 and 350. The Blue Lick Well was discovered in 1888 by Curtis Benjamin "CB" Lore. Lore was a well driller from Pennsylvania who, along with others in his crew, accidentally discovered the well while they were drilling the area looking for gas. Lore was married to Jacob Kirsch's daughter Nora. For many years, the well was thought to have special healing properties and powers. People would come from miles around to bathe in water from the well.

Physicians during the time were said to even send their patients to get water from the well. The well was believed to have the power to cure everything from eczema to stomach ailments. The town built a small pavilion so that people could be covered while using the water. Unfortunately, the pavilion was destroyed in the 1937 flood, and the well was not the same after that.

Today, there is a brick-covered structure where the well was once located. This structure was built in 1966 as a way to remember the Blue Lick Well.

BRIARWAY NORTH DRIVE

In the fall of 2003, Rebecca and Earl Wilhelm began looking for a home for their growing family. The family had their sights set on building a modular home on a piece of land out in the country. They were hoping for peace, quiet and a comfortable place to build a family. That is not what they got, however.

The couple picked out a home from the Riverside Home Sales, located at that time on US 50 in Aurora. They settled on a three-bedroom and two-bathroom model with an open floor plan that seemed perfect for their needs. Burgundy carpeting, a kitchen with so much counter and cabinet space and a master bedroom with its own en suite bathroom made the home seem to be something out of a dream. Earl and Rebecca picked out this model, and then the search began for a piece of land on which to have the house placed.

The owner of the home sales company had a piece of land that he thought would be perfect. It was located in Manchester Township on Briarway North Drive. The land and spot were just that, perfect.

Earl and Rebecca moved into the home in February 2004 when their son was a baby. During the first few weeks in the house, everything seemed to be normal. However, it was not long before weird things started occurring. The first thing that happened was the heavy footsteps in the kitchen. Earl worked the night shift, and in the early mornings as Rebecca lay in bed, she would hear footsteps as if someone had entered the kitchen and was walking around. Rebecca got up and walked to the bedroom door. From there, she could see the kitchen back door reflected from the hallway bathroom mirror. No one was ever there. The footsteps always stopped just as Rebecca reached the bedroom door.

Another strange event happened one night when Rebecca was in the kitchen washing dishes. She had put the baby to bed and turned on some music while she washed up and straightened up the house. As she stood at the sink, she heard a small voice say, "Mommy." At first, she thought it was a noise on the radio. She turned down the music and listened. She heard nothing.

Thinking it must have been something on the radio, Rebecca turned the music back up and continued her tasks. After a few minutes, she heard the small voice say, "Mommy" again. This time, the hair on her arms stood up. She quickly said, "I'm not your Mommy." She finished her work, checked on the baby and went back to her bedroom to watch television and go to bed.

The sounds of horses were sometimes heard outside of the house late at night. Several times, Earl and Rebecca heard the sounds of horses. It sounded as if there were lots of horses running through the yard and right outside of the house. Thinking it was just the neighbor's animals, they would look outside to see nothing there.

The next odd occurrence would be something that many other visitors to the house would experience. Late at night, if the window in the third bedroom was opened, you could hear talking going on from outside. It sounded like a woman, a man and a small child. The man and woman sounded as if they were arguing. This would go on for several minutes. It would stop whenever someone would get up to check to see if anyone was outside of the window. Visitors to the house did not want to sleep in the third bedroom.

Another strange incident that happened in the home concerns the Wilhelms' son, Earl George. He started seeing what he referred to as a "ghost boy." Here is an account of Earl's experience with the spirit he called the ghost boy and his mommy:

My room and my sister's room were in a hallway to the right when you walked in, and my parents to the left. This is important. At the time, I was about five, so a lot scared me. This really messed me up for years though. I had a little shelf with toy trains on it. It was right at the foot of my bed. I woke up in the middle of the night to see a slightly transparent little boy playing with my trains. Then he just disappeared. Remember when I told you where the rooms are? I got up and ran across the living room practically having a panic attack just to look into my kitchen and see what must have been the child's mother, also transparent. I ran into my parents' room, dolphin dived into the bed and woke my parents up. This happened a few times with different objects until we finally moved out three years later.

The Wilhelms and visitors to their home started experiencing seeing something out of the corner of their eyes while seated on the couch. While watching television, people started reporting seeing a glimpse of a small child running back and forth to the bedrooms in the hallway. Over the six years that the Wilhelms lived in the home, several people had this experience.

Earl George's sister, Hope, also had an experience in the house when she was very young. Early one morning, she got up and was playing with her toys before waking up her parents. Suddenly, the bedroom door slammed shut, and she could not get it opened. Hope said that a lady appeared in the room and opened the door for her. "She told me that there was a really mean ghost in my house and that I needed to get my mommy." Looking through family pictures once, Hope pointed to a picture of Rebecca's great-grandmother Jenny and identified her as the woman who let her out of the bedroom that day.

The last straw for the Wilhelm family came when one evening Rebecca; her sister Mary; their mother, Ellen; and a family friend, Crystal, were sitting around the dining room table. All of a sudden, Ellen started pointing to Earl George's bedroom. She said she saw an unseen something pulling the covers and dragging Earl George from his bed. Horrified, Rebecca took him out of his bed and put him to bed in the living room. The Wilhelms contacted their pastor, who came and did a blessing on their home. Curiously, the activities in this home stopped.

Nothing was ever heard again until the Wilhelms moved out of the home. They had moved everything but a few items and their pets. Rebecca came back to the house to get the pets and the items. While using the restroom in the master bedroom, she once again heard heavy footsteps in the kitchen area. She quickly collected the pets and walked out of the door. She never looked back to see if anything was there.

7

BIG CAT OF DEARBORN COUNTY

W hen a person thinks of wild or exotic cats, Indiana is not the first place that comes to mind. In fact, according to the Indiana Department of Natural Resources, the bobcat is the only native wild cat in the state. However, over the years, Indiana residents, specifically those in Dearborn County, have reported numerous sightings of a wild cat in the area that mysteriously disappears. There are many theories about what this cat may be, but so far, no one has been able to figure it out. In order to explain why these sightings are so unique, let us first understand what kinds of wild cats have roamed the backwoods of this beautiful state.

Although known for being elusive, bobcats are not a rare thing to see in Indiana. Early settlers to the state would have been familiar with this nocturnal creature, as the population was considerable at the time. Bobcats love wooded areas and prefer to stay far away from people. They mostly dine on rabbits or mice and have been known to snack on a stray chicken or two. There have been sightings in almost every county of the state. However, the bobcat is most common in central and southern Indiana. It was such a commonality in local wildlife that Moores Hill Elementary School chose the bobcat as its school mascot when it opened in 1987.

As the state's population grew, bobcats became almost extinct in Indiana. They were added to the endangered species list in 1970, but these popular cats returned due to the hard work of conservationists. By 2005, the population was considered stable and no longer endangered. The Indiana Department of Natural Resources, or Indiana DNR, closely tracks

County Line Road between Ripley and Dearborn County. Motorists in the area have experienced close calls with a mysterious cat that runs across the road.

Field with hay bales in Moores Hill, Indiana. A wild cat has been seen running through the fields of Dearborn County for over a century.

the bobcat population. With the use of implanted tracking devices and trail cameras, they keep an eye on where these animals are congregating in the state. However, no one is quite sure how big the total population may be. Even without the tracking devices, one can be sure the numbers have increased based on the high frequency of recent sightings and the unfortunate number of bobcats being hit by vehicles across the state.

Outside of the bobcat, the Indiana DNR does not recognize any other wild cat species as being native to the state. Mountain lions once lived throughout most of the eastern United States. However, as people moved west, the U.S. government sent large groups of hunters to several states to kill off these large populations. At the time, it was to protect settlers in the area from being attacked. Because of this, Indiana has had no significant mountain lion population since the 1880s. This does not mean they completely disappeared.

An article from the *Indy Star* newspaper in 2014 mentioned that the Indiana DNR had "received about 300 reports of big cat sightings since early 2010." Most of these were thought to be mountain lions based on the description of markings and the size of the cat seen. One sighting even came from a police officer in southwestern Indiana, near Bedford, who saw a mountain lion eating a deer along IN State Road 37. The Indiana DNR confirmed a few of the sightings but claimed these were likely young male mountain lions passing through to other areas of the country. Others were thought to be bobcats, misconstrued as mountain lions or people making up encounters for internet fame.

Out of all the wild cats that exist in the United States, a panther, specifically a black panther, is the most unlikely wild cat to be found in southeast Indiana. This is where the mysterious tales of the "Big Cat of Dearborn County" begin.

A black panther is a form of leopard that is actually not native to the United States at all. The species originally comes from tropical forests, such as those found in India, Africa and South America. There have been sightings of panthers in the southern parts of the United States, but most of these have been debunked over time as other forms of wild cats. The ones that have been confirmed stem from zoo animals that got loose at some point in time or those kept as pets that were released into the wild. Considering that leopards thrive in warmer climates, it is difficult to understand how they could survive in the harsh winters of Indiana. However, sightings of a black panther roaming around Dearborn County, and other parts of Indiana, have been reported since the mid-1800s.

According to the website *An Unnatural History of Indiana,* by Tim Swartz, one of the first recorded encounters happened in 1877 when a young couple walking home one evening was chased by a large cat "as big as a good-sized calf." The cat pinned the girl to the ground and licked her face, only to disappear into the night. There was also what was described as a "black mountain lion" that terrorized residents in the southern part of the state from 1908 to 1910. It would chase or attack residents, only coming out at night. There were notices put in the newspapers at the time reminding people to carry guns when going out after dark. Both instances were thought to be real-life cats because of the paw prints left behind at the scene. However, in the 1940s, the sightings became more sinister.

Throughout the 1940s, farmers in southern Indiana and parts of Dearborn County lost livestock to an animal they described as a "cat as black as night." Several farmers lost entire fields of livestock at a time, which was costly and distressing in an area that depended on farming. One farmer complained to the local sheriff about the oddity of the killings. He lost seven hogs, all killed by a large black cat that ate their hearts and livers. Another farmer lost a goat, three hogs and a calf in the same manner—only in his case, the hearts were removed and the blood drained from the bodies. Farmers across the state described the cat the same way: a large black cat with glowing red eyes and huge claws. The glowing red eyes quickly started the rumor of this being a demonic cat or a ghost cat.

Sightings in Dearborn County died by 1948, but the mysterious cat did not leave the state. There continued to be attacks and sightings all over Indiana, and almost no county was left untouched. The most notorious black panther encounters were in Noblesville in 1951, Monument City in 1952 and as far north as Michigan City and La Porte in 1954.

In 1956, Mrs. Arthur Hamon shared an experience with the *Dearborn County Register* that happened at her home on Morgan Road near Bright. One evening when her son was at home alone, he heard the dog start to growl. Looking out the window, he saw a catlike creature about "three feet long and between 15 and 18 inches tall," resembling a panther. The cat attacked the dog, which prompted her son to run inside and grab his gun. Once he returned outside, the cat was gone. Thankfully, the dog suffered only minor injuries. This was one of many experiences that happened in the area that year.

A year later, in September 1957, the *Lawrenceburg Press* printed a reminder to residents to watch their animals. At the time, several homes lost chickens and other small farm animals to a reported catlike creature in the area. It was thought to be a vicious strain of housecat gone wild from an owner letting it loose to fend for itself. Some people believed it could be a house cat that mated with a bobcat. Others thought it could be a descendant of a cat let loose after the alleged train derailment at the Bonnell Train Bridge in Guilford, Indiana. The train was said to be carrying either wild animals or circus animals. The most likely explanation was that several homes and businesses were being built in the 1950s, so it was thought to possibly be a wild cat brought into town due to the loss of its habitat.

After the spurt of sightings in the 1950s, activity in Dearborn County lessened, and most encounters were noted in the central and northern parts of the state. Numerous stories came out of La Porte, Indiana, in the 1980s. Several of these ended up noted in police reports at the time. However, in the 1990s, this unusual cat returned to southeastern Indiana.

In August 1995, a resident of nearby Batesville was returning home from work one evening when he had an encounter that changed his opinion of these stories forever. As he turned down his long driveway, he noticed a large black cat walking along the end of the drive near the house. The man was

The Bonnell Train Bridge in Guilford, Indiana. This is the site of an alleged train derailment that may have carried animals.

immediately spooked but became even more so as he got closer to the cat. Once halfway down the drive, he realized that the cat was not solid. Instead, it was the shadow of a cat in the form of a giant panther. He could see the trees along the property line through the shape of the cat. It paid no attention to his car nearing the home. In fact, the cat walked toward the house, disappearing into the side. The man notified local law enforcement officers, but no one was able to find signs of a large cat in the area.

A similar encounter happened near Aurora in the early 2000s when a woman looked out her window to see a large cat running across her lawn. It was making loud growling and hissing sounds. Terrified, the woman closed all her blinds and locked the doors to wait until the cat left. The cat continued to wander in her and the neighbor's yard for about two hours, when it suddenly ran from the area. Like the Batesville experience, the cat was described as being transparent and not a solid creature. It also had the glowing red eyes mentioned in many previous cases. There were no signs of paw prints or worn grass where the cat was pacing from the night before. The woman never had another encounter with the animal after that night. To date, this is the only encounter that involves the cat vocalizing.

There were several encounters in the 2000s of people almost hitting panther-like creatures when driving in the area. One was from a schoolteacher driving to work early in the morning when a panther ran across the road. She swerved to miss the large cat, almost driving off the road in the process. She called the police, who searched for a wild cat for weeks after the incident. Nothing was ever found.

There was also a situation with a local law enforcement officer who was driving on patrol one evening when a large panther ran in front of his patrol car. Unable to swerve out of the way, the officer hit the cat. He could feel the impact of the collision so strong that it caused the car to jerk and abruptly come to a stop. Expecting the worst, the officer got out of the car to find that there was no cat to be found. Not only that, but there was no damage to the car at all. There were no paw prints, blood or signs that he hit anything.

With the most recent encounters, most residents in the area have started to shift their beliefs of a wild cat gone unnoticed to the possibility of a ghost or demon cat roaming the area. While ghost cats are not common in local legends and folklore, they are found in other areas of the world. Most cultures have some version of a mythical cat, and some of the legends have immigrated to the United States with the people who brought them here.

One example is the Yule Cat, or the Christmas Cat, from Iceland. This large black cat arrives on Christmas to eat children who did not receive new clothes to wear for the coming year. This may sound odd at first, but the idea is that children who failed to receive new clothes on Christmas must have been naughty the year before. Not getting clothes is the equivalent of getting coal in your stocking. Although this cat is described as being large, it in no way resembles the cat described in Dearborn County. Also, the sightings do not revolve around any specific holiday.

There is the cat-sith from Scotland, which is a black fairy cat that is depicted as large as a dog. According to legends, the cat steals a person's soul after they pass before God can take it. This is where we get the tradition of having a wake when someone dies. "People would watch a corpse day and night to keep the cat-sith from sneaking up before burial," according to an online article about mythical cats by Chelsie Fraser. The Big Cat of Dearborn County does not appear to be attracted to death or corpses.

Other examples are the Carbunclo, or Carbuncle, a black cat from Chile that guards metal in the mining communities. This cat is described as being small, which differs from what is seen in Indiana. It is also said to have green eyes and glow as though being lit from within. There is the Kasha, a black demon cat from Japan that is known to steal corpses. This is why some areas of Japan perform two funerals when someone dies. The first funeral is used as a decoy to keep the real body from being stolen. There is also the Magatot from southern France. This is a black spirit cat that will bring good luck to those who feed it and bad luck to those who do not. While all of these may share physical similarities with the cat seen in Indiana, none of them make sense with the activity surrounding its actions.

The most similar cat from folklore that fits the one seen in Indiana would be the Cha Kla. This legend from Thailand was first spoken about in American culture in 1907. The Cha Kla is a black cat with thick, matted fur that grows back to front. It is known for its glowing red eyes and vicious nature. The cat acts under the command of a jungle sorcerer who uses the cat to attack enemies. It is fearful of humans and will hide from them unless on a killing mission. Legend says that the cat will disappear from view by jumping into a magical hole in the ground. However, if a person comes in contact with the Cha Kla, they will die shortly after. One legend from the early 1900s speaks of the death of a man's son from dysentery due to touching this mysterious cat a few days before. Could Dearborn County's mysterious big cat be our very own version of the Cha Kla? The two certainly share many similarities, which would explain why the cat disappears and is never found.

Indiana continues to deal with cat encounters throughout the state. Some are real cats, and some remain unexplained. It is not uncommon to hear of farmers losing livestock or people encountering mysterious-looking cats while walking local trails or hunting. The disappearing black cat of Dearborn County also still appears from time to time. Each year, someone new will share their encounter, prompting people from all over the county to share their experiences. What is the big cat of Dearborn County? Is it a new, unidentified species living in the rural areas of our state? Could it be a mythical creature sent to wreak havoc on unsuspecting residents? Perhaps we will never know.

8

LOST SOULS OF THE DEARBORN COUNTY JAIL

It should come as no surprise that a jail would be the location of several hauntings—especially when you consider the number of people that go through the doors each day and are responsible for some of the most heinous crimes in the area. It makes sense that these tortured souls, or the ones they harmed, would stick around one of the last places they inhabited and make their presence known. Almost every law enforcement officer that has worked at the Dearborn County Jail has experienced the paranormal. Most are too scared to talk about it, but those who have shared stories that would shake the biggest skeptic.

The current jail is one of a long line of jails built for the county. The building of a jail was prompted due to an altercation between a judge and a person serving as a witness in the court. Apparently, the two got into an argument that resulted in the judge's arms being broken. The witness was found to be in contempt of court and "was ordered to jail, but there was no jail" according to the book *History of Dearborn and Ohio Counties, Indiana*. The first one was built in 1804 in Lawrenceburg. The building was made from logs and was on the public square in the middle of town. The first jailer to live on the premises was William Cook, who lived there in 1806.

The second jail was built sometime around 1827, presumably due to needing a more stable structure. There is little mention of the second jail in historical documents. In the *State Gazetteer* of 1833, it is referred to as a stone jail. It is also recorded as being two stories high, the first of its kind for the area.

The 1870 Dearborn County Courthouse adjacent to the Dearborn County Law Enforcement Center.

In 1835, the county seat was moved from Lawrenceburg to Wilmington. At the time, Ohio County did not exist. Wilmington was considered a more geographically central location for the area, and people at the time were hoping this would help keep better control of county resources. With the move came a new courthouse and jail. They were built on land owned by the local Masonic Lodge. This building only survived a few years before being damaged by fire. The building was replaced in 1840 in the same location, making this the fourth jail.

In 1848, the county seat moved back to Lawrenceburg. A fifth jail was once again built on the public square. As mentioned in *History of Dearborn and Ohio Counties, Indiana*, the building was made of stone with a special provision "for the building of a wall above the high water mark of 1832." The flood of 1832 was the worst recorded flood in history for this area at the time. The Ohio River was known for flooding, but this particular flood had water about seven feet higher than the highest recorded flood prior to this. Most homes in the area suffered damage, and many buildings were wiped away from their foundations. The goal was to build a jail that would withstand another natural disaster of this magnitude.

Unfortunately, it would not be the last jail.

A sixth jail was built between 1858 and 1859. This time, the building was again two stories and included a home for the sheriff. The home faced High Street, and the jail was in the rear of the house. The inner door between the buildings was thick and weighed eight hundred pounds in order to keep the sheriff and his wife safe from criminals. This remained the jail until 1954, when the building became too dilapidated to stay in use. A 1954 newspaper article from the *Lawrenceburg Press* mentions that "cracked walls and unsanitary conditions feature its deteriorating condition."

The changing of technology and tools also caused the jail to become obsolete. It became known in the area as being "easy to get into and easy to break out of," as mentioned in an article by *Register Publications* in 2020. In September 1954, seven inmates attempted to escape the jail by using hacksaw blades to saw through the bars of their cells. The hacksaw blades were snuck into the jail by visitors, and inmates would saw when trains were passing by to help eliminate the sound. Luckily, law enforcement officers were notified of the plan and were able to stop them before they accomplished their goal. This was the final straw that encouraged the building of the seventh jail.

Very little information is known about the seventh jail, but we do know that the eighth jail was built in 1975. It served the area for six years before it quickly became overcrowded. As the area continued to grow in population and crime reached levels not seen before, Dearborn County found itself unable to house all the criminals. They would have to transport inmates to nearby Brookville or Madison, which was becoming costly to the county.

In 1981, then sheriff James Wismann began petitioning for a larger, more updated jail. Due to changes made to state policy, the jail was unable to meet all of the requirements due to a lack of space. They would be required to have special cells for persons under the influence of drugs or alcohol and padded cells for violent persons. They also had to implement audiovisual equipment in each cell for monitoring. This did not take into account overcrowding at the jail, which was already the main issue. After several years of presenting facts and reasoning to county commissioners, the sheriff was eventually given permission to build an addition to the current jail or make updates to the building. It took another decade before the approval of an all-new law enforcement facility was given.

The current jail is ninth on the list of Dearborn County jails. It was built between 1990 and 1991 at 301 West High Street in order to once again combat overcrowding at the previous jail. It was a $10 million project that increased the capacity of the jail from 32 inmates to 120 inmates, according to an article in the *Dearborn County Register* from 1990. The new design also

The Dearborn County Jail, the site of several unexplained paranormal experiences by officers and inmates alike.

Juvenile Center, Dearborn County Jail and courthouse. Located on High Street in Lawrenceburg, Indiana.

formed a complete law enforcement center that houses the Dearborn County Sheriff's Department, a communication center where emergency calls are received and a tunnel connecting the jail to the courthouse for easy transport of prisoners to court. There was also a juvenile building added in 1993.

The stories of creepy happenings at the current jail began right from the start. One of the first prisoners to ever stay in the building was William Hardebeck, who was housed in the jail due to Ripley County's jail being full. Hardebeck murdered five of his family members, including his mother, three siblings and a brother-in-law. He claimed demons made him commit the murders and that the demons had followed him to jail. Hardebeck was later found guilty but mentally ill and was sentenced to 240 years in prison.

Unfortunately, the demons at the jail appear not to have left with Hardebeck. Over the years, inmates have claimed to hear voices telling them to do things and complained about the constant whispering in their ears. Others claim that the demons taunt them and encourage them to harm other people at the jail. There have also been sightings of a shadow figure with glowing red eyes. Whether these demons exist is purely speculation, but one has to wonder about the connection.

The more common ghostly occurrences around the jail involve less scary origins. One encounter happened in the early 2000s with Dearborn County officer Earl Wilhelm. Officer Wilhelm was working an overnight shift on Control 1, which is a high tower overlooking the rest of the jail. During his shift, he developed an uneasy feeling of being watched. At the time, no one else was working in the area, but the feeling was persistent. After a while, he looked out the windows to find a figure in white staring at him from outside. The figure appeared to be floating in mid-air, and it disappeared once noticed by Officer Wilhelm. There was no way this could be a real person because it was several feet in the air where there was no access point.

Another active part of the jail is the showers, where an unseen ghost likes to play with the shower curtains. One evening, Officer Wilhelm was doing evening rounds and checking the shower stalls as part of the process. He walked through the area with all shower curtains opened where he could see into the stall and make sure no one was hiding. When walking back through the shower area, he found all shower curtains closed. No one else was in the area, especially since he had just cleared it.

Another officer experienced this same shower curtain phenomenon. He also walked through during routine evening rounds. Only in this situation, the shower curtains were already closed. When walking by, he could hear and see the shower curtains behind him open and sway as though being hit by an invisible person following him down the hallway. Most officers have experienced the shower curtains moving during the evening rounds, and inmates claim to have an uneasy feeling of being watched as they bathe.

Other occurrences at the jail include the sound of footsteps. Officers have reported the sound of running or loud walking down the halls of the jail. However, cameras pick up no physical person in the area, and no one is found when searching the area. One officer had a terrifying experience of hearing running footsteps behind him one night. They were loud enough to make him believe he was about to be attacked. Bracing himself to be hit, he turned around to find there was no one behind him. Only a rush of air blasted past him, making the hair on his arms stand up. There was no one else in the hallway.

Most of the hauntings appear to be seen by officers and other members of law enforcement. There have also been several suicides on the premises by inmates over the years. Because of this, the most common theory is that the hauntings are caused by former inmates who never left after their passing. Whether demons or former inmates, one cannot help but wonder who haunts the Dearborn County Jail.

9

SPIRITS OF LOCHRY'S DEFEAT

When you think of the Revolutionary War, you tend to think of the original thirteen colonies and all the many battles that happened along the East Coast. Most people do not realize that Indiana was also an important part of the Revolutionary War. In fact, one noteworthy battle happened in Dearborn County right along the Ohio River.

Indiana was still considered part of the frontier at the time, and the Ohio River Valley suffered numerous attacks from Native American tribes near Detroit supported by the British. To keep the fur trade attached to the British Empire, the British army convinced the Native Americans that the colonists were not to be trusted and supplied their tribes with ammunition and materials needed to fight off the invaders.

George Rogers Clark, a well-known Virginia militia officer, believed that a sure way of winning the region was by overcoming the threat in Detroit. He met with then Virginia governor Thomas Jefferson to devise a plan to lead two thousand men to battle in the area.

In January 1781, Clark set out to Pennsylvania to acquire a group of men and supplies. During this task, he met Colonel Archibald Lochry, a commander from Westmoreland County. Clark needed help recruiting men due to lingering arguments between Virginia and Pennsylvania over the border. He thought that having Lochry lead the men in his place would ensure their cooperation. When Clark finally left the area in August, he had recruited only about four hundred men.

The site of Lochry's defeat, a Revolutionary War battle that changed Indiana's history forever. Laughery Creek, Aurora, Indiana.

Unfortunately, the British army became aware of Clark's plan early in the year, giving them plenty of time to develop a counterattack. An official council to plan a defense was held in Detroit in April. They spent the next few months recruiting leaders from the Six Nations of the Iroquois Confederacy. One such leader was Joseph Brant (also known as Thayendanegea), a leader of the Mohawks. In August, Brant led a group of ninety warriors south to the Ohio River to head off any attacks from Clark, Lochry and their men.

Around the same time, Clark took off with his men by boat down the Ohio River with the idea that Lochry and his group meet up with them. However, the two groups kept missing each other. Clark would leave notes to let Lochry and his men know where to go next. He would also leave provisions that were often missing when Lochry arrived at a post. Unfortunately, this took a toll on both parties, and Lochry's team eventually began to run out of food and supplies.

One note from Lochry read:

> *My dear General. I arrived at this Post this moment. I find that there is neither Boats, provisions or ammunition left. I have sent a small canoe after you to know what is to be done.*

Lochry's defeat historical marker. Located outside of the Triple Whipple Bridge next to Laughery Creek.

On the night of August 18, Cark finally made his way to where the Ohio River meets the border between Ohio and Indiana at the mouth of what is now known as Laughery Creek. Brant and his men hid on the north shore but decided not to attack Clark and his men due to being out of reinforcements and not having a full team. They had sent men out to get supplies earlier in the day and needed more people to launch an ambush successfully. Brant knew that Lochry would soon follow, so he waited for them to arrive. Most people are unaware of how close Clark came to losing his life that day, especially considering his importance to Indiana history.

On the morning of August 24, Lochry's group landed on the river's north shore after being lured ashore by Brant. It is said that Lochry's carelessness caused the success of this ambush. Even though he knew the chance of being attacked was high, he landed to feed his men and horses without taking proper precautions. Brant fired on the party, taking the Americans by surprise. Most members of the party didn't even have their weapons on them, and those that did quickly ran out of ammunition. Seeing no hope of winning, Lochry ordered his men to surrender.

Triple Whipple Bridge between Dearborn and Ohio Counties, crossing Laughery Creek, as seen from US 56.

Almost all of the Americans were either killed or captured. Very few of Brant's men were injured. According to records, thirty-seven Americans were killed, and sixty-four were captured. Most of those that survived were executed afterward, including Lochry, who was killed by a Shawnee warrior.

Although we attribute this battle to Indiana's history, it is crucial to realize its impact on Westmoreland County, Pennsylvania. Almost every home in the county was affected by losing a loved one. Most families were unaware of the deaths until December, when General William Irvine sent a letter to Fort Pitt in Pittsburgh. Even worse, the county lost its strongest soldiers, leaving the rest of the area without defense. Most of the dead were never returned home, and many were buried near the site of what is now known as River View Cemetery.

While the battle was long ago, the traces of this event are still evident all over Dearborn County. Both Laughery Creek and the road of the same name are named after Lochry. Unfortunately, the name has been misspelled many times over the years. The book *History of Dearborn and Ohio Counties, Indiana* mentions that "in Dillon's History of Indiana, it is written Loughry; in Collin's History of Kentucky, Loughrey, although in the Annals of Kentucky, prefixed to the latter work, we have Lochry and Lochiy's Creek." Charles Martindale's account of the battle in Indiana Historical Society publications misspelled the name as Laughery, and the paperwork to name the road was sent in as such. Thus, it remains this way today. Historical markers on Old State Road 56 commemorate the battle's historical significance, and a memorial for all lost lives is also located in River View Cemetery nearby.

Triple Whipple Bridge between Dearborn and Ohio Counties. Motorists crossing the bridge are said to see mysterious, ghostly lights on the ground below.

With such a large number of deaths and the historical importance of the battle, it is easy to imagine that these lost souls have never left. Residents have claimed to hear the sounds of horses running near where the battle happened, but upon investigation, there are no horses in sight. There have also been reports of hearing what sounds like soldiers marching from a distance. Visitors to River View Cemetery have heard the sounds of yelling and crying near the memorial.

One common occurrence involves the Triple Whipple Bridge, also known as the Laughery Creek Bridge, which was built in 1878. When walking over the bridge, people claim to see eerie, ghostly lights floating near the edges of the creek. These do not follow the patterns of bugs flying or animals. Instead, they all move at different paces, some zig-zagging fast and others slowly moving along. A team of local ghost hunters experienced what they thought was a floating head when investigating the bridge late one evening. The way the bridge is built would make it impossible for someone to be walking along the outside of the structure.

One resident, who wishes to remain anonymous, claims to have seen shadow figures walking alongside the creek one evening. As they neared the figures, they observed that they were see-through and quickly realized that these were not real people. As they neared the spot, the shadow figures disappeared. Could these be the men still trying to find their way home?

The events of this battle are often overlooked in Indiana history, and many do not realize that such an important event happened right in their backyard. The official commemoration of the memorial in 1924 drew little recognition. This upset Dearborn County resident Archibald Shaw, who wrote a letter of complaint to the *Indianapolis Star* in June of that year: "Not as much attention as it deserves has been given to this event in Indiana history, really the only battle fought on Indiana soil during the revolutionary war, the siege and capture of Vincennes being a bloodless affair in comparison." Thankfully, the people of Dearborn County have not forgotten the sacrifice these men gave in the pursuit of freedom.

10

THE AURORA PUBLIC LIBRARY

T he City of Aurora was founded in 1819. Shortly after, plans were made to establish a library. The Aurora Public Library was organized, and a lot was purchased on what is now Fifth Street. It was originally known as Literary Street because of the intention to have the library there.

Gathering the funds to build a library building proved extremely difficult for the small river town. The library was first housed in various residences and eventually in a downtown jewelry store. In 1901, the library was operating out of two rooms in the Aurora city building on Third Street. The library had grown to have a collection of 3,500 books and materials. While the library was operating out of the city building, it was able to be open for three afternoons and two evenings per week.

The Aurora Public Library that we know today was built on the old Siemental Property on Second Street in downtown Aurora. Siemental means "cattle," so it had been land that cows were on. The land was purchased with money that was donated by Georgiana Sutton in 1913. Construction began, and the building was completed in 1914. A rear addition was built in 1924. The side additions were added in 1997, and the basement has undergone several renovations to house the children's section, computers, library offices and the downstairs circulation desk.

Library founder Georgiana Sutton was the daughter of the famous early Aurora physician Dr. George Sutton. Dr. Sutton, who is referred to by many as a pioneer doctor, was actually much more than that. Sutton was instrumental in the study of epidemics in Indiana in the nineteenth century.

Above: The Aurora Public Library was built in 1913 due to a generous gift from benefactor Georgianna Sutton.

Right: Cardboard cutout displayed at the library in honor of benefactor Georgianna Sutton, whose gift made the library possible.

Dedication to Dr. and Mrs. Sutton. V is used as U, as in the Latin alphabet, which was common in nineteenth- and early twentieth-century building features.

Georgiana never married, and she was a well-traveled and well-educated woman. She inherited a lot of money from her parents when they passed.

What Georgiana wanted more than anything was to honor her parents with a public library built in their memory. Upon her death in 1910, she put aside $10,000 for the purchase of the library. As you enter the library, there is a plaque above the door honoring her beloved father and mother.

The library has been rumored to be haunted for many years. According to one of the Aurora Public Library historians, the rumors of the origin of the library being haunted and the ghost stories may trace back to Native American spirits. According to an October 13, 2017 Aurora Public Library blog post, an 1885 archaeological publication reported "a large Indian mound in downtown Aurora that was partially destroyed when the streets were originally graded." The blog notes that the only area of downtown Aurora that is mounded is the land where the library sits today.

Dr. George Sutton was what we would today call a relic hunter. He held a strong interest in recording Native American history and wrote several papers about the Native Americans that once lived in the area. The October 13, 2017 blog post points out that apparently, when grading was done on what is now Mechanic Street, Indian bones were discovered. Dr. Sutton was well known for having a large collection of various Native American artifacts. The Mechanic Street bones were added to his collection. One of the former library staff said that these bones from Dr. Sutton's collection were originally stored in the basement of the library.

On January 26, 1937, one of the very worst floods to ever hit Aurora occurred. The Ohio River, on this day, reached a stage of eighty feet. The entire town ended up being affected. The Aurora Public Library had six inches of water in its upstairs. Thankfully, none of the items in storage in the basement were damaged. As the waters inched closer and closer to the library, items were moved elsewhere for safekeeping.

As a result, the library did not lose any of its materials to floodwaters. However, Dr. Sutton's collection was part of the materials that were moved. After the flood, the library never saw the bones again. No one knows exactly what happened to them or where they are today.

There is some interesting ghost lore associated with the library. The most well-known story about the library revolves around the upstairs main library doors and is reported on the library's blog. Many of the library staff over the years have reported a strange occurrence when they are opening the upstairs doors. When you open the doors, you will find that one of the doors will open by itself. It will do this each time.

Another well-known phenomenon is the lady in black. Seen by many of the staff over decades, she is seen just out of the corner of the eye. The lady in black is always seen upstairs in the original part of the building. People have caught a quick glimpse of a lady in a long black dress walking

The main upstairs Aurora Public Library doors that seem to open mysteriously.

quickly between the shelving. Is this the spirit of the first librarian, or is it possibly Georgiana Sutton?

One death did occur upstairs in 1922. According to one of the library historians, an elderly patron fell asleep and did not wake up. Local legend says that this patron did not have family and spent his days at the library, considering the library staff to be his family. To this day, the library has a policy of not allowing sleeping. This policy stemmed from this incident. Many have felt as if the man's spirit is still there. Cold spots have been reported, and it is thought that this is the elderly patron's spirit.

Passersby have felt like they see people in the library after hours. Many stories circulate of people thinking they see someone in the library windows after hours. There is an eerie feeling in the evening when you walk past the building.

According to the library blog, a paranormal group was brought in to investigate some of the reported hauntings back in 2015. The group did experience some things that they felt meant that the library may be haunted. The group caught some orbs, cold spots and feelings of being watched. The group did get some interaction involving some of their equipment in the building, especially the basement area, where Dr. Sutton's collection was stored so many years ago.

THE OLD AURORA TRAIN DEPOT

At 414 Second Street in Aurora, an old train depot stands next to the railroad tracks. It is a red brick structure with a tiled roof. It was purchased in 2008 by the Aurora Public Library District. Since that time, it has operated as the local history library. The local history library contains history from Aurora and the surrounding area that dates to 1836.

The current building we know today was constructed in 1916 by the Baltimore and Ohio Railroad and is actually the second train depot building to have been constructed on the site. After many floods in Aurora, the original building was damaged and needed to be replaced. The first depot was built in 1854 by the Mississippi and Ohio Railroad. Its purpose was for the train that ran daily between Cincinnati, Ohio, and Cochran, Indiana.

The last train to the depot was in 1976. Between then and the purchase by the library, the depot operated as shops. One patron recalled a flower shop being in the depot at one time. It was a gift shop as well.

Old Train Depot in Aurora, Indiana. It now serves as the Local History Library and is the main source of genealogical information for the area.

For over 122 years, many people passed through the depot. One of the local legends about the depot concerns a robbery that occurred shortly after the depot's 1916 construction. According to a former local library staff member, a conductor was robbed and put into the cellar basement one evening. He was told not to try to escape or to look out or else they would kill him. He was found later and escaped unharmed. The librarian was told this by the great-grandson of the conductor when he came by the depot one day for a visit.

Today, former employees have reported hearing sounds like someone moving around in the cellar basement. There have been reported sounds as if the heavy door was slammed shut when the door has not been moved. There have also been lighting issues where lights turn off or go back on seemingly with a mind of their own. The classic cold spots or feelings of staff being watched when they are all alone in the building have been recorded.

What or who is the spirit lingering at the Aurora Public Library and local library depot? Maybe someday we'll know for sure.

BIBLIOGRAPHY

Aukepalmhof. "Forest Queen USS Transport." Ship Stamp Society, March 6, 2016. https://shipstamps.co.uk.

Aurora (IN) Bulletin. "Five Members of Family Slain." Thursday, May 22, 1941. Courtesy of the Aurora Public Library.

Bloodgood, Don E. "Early Health Conditions in Indiana." Purdue University, Lafayette, Indiana, 1951. https://journals.iupui.edu/index.php/ias/article/download/5807/5792/.

Cahill, Lora Schmidt. *Thunderbolt: Revisit Southeastern Indiana with John Hunt Morgan.* Attica, OH: K-Hill Publishing, 1995.

Cincinnati (OH) Enquirer. "Still Wife of Accused Killer." October 18, 1941. https://www.newspapers.com.

Cincinnati USA. "Hillforest Mansion." July 2, 2022. https://cincinnatiusa.com.

City of Aurora. "Dr. George Sutton." https://aurora.in.us/bicentennial-history.html.

CNN. "Flooding Peak Is Past; Now, the Cleanup Starts." March 7, 1997. http://www.cnn.com.

Daily Reporter (Greenfield, IN). "Suspect Faces Lie Detector Test." May 19, 1941. https://www.newspapers.com.

Dearborn County. "County History." https://www.dearborncounty.org.

Eagle 99.3 News. "Demolition Begins at Old North Dearborn Elementary School." December 22, 2021. https://www.eaglecountryonline.com.

Estes, Roberta. "Jacob Kirsch (1841–1917), Lynching Saloonist with a Glass Eye, 52 Ancestors #109." *DNA Explained,* January 31, 2016. https://dna-explained.com.

Evening Independent (Massillon, OH). "Arrested in Death Quiz." May 20, 1941. https://www.newspapers.com.

Fraser, Chelsie. "25 Cats from Mythology—Exploring the World of Mythical Cats." *Hepper,* February 23, 2023. https://www.hepper.com/cats-from-mythology/.

Greensburg (IN) Daily News. "Robbery Hinted as Possible Motive for Family Slaughter Near Aurora." May 19, 1941. https://www.newspapers.com.

Hillforest Victorian House Museum. "History." https://hillforest.org/history.

History.com Editors. "Andrew Carnegie." History.com, November 9, 2009. https://www.history.com.

History in Your Own Backyard. "North Dearborn High School, Dover, Indiana." YouTube, May 23, 2022. https://youtu.be/2ukq3g3gsQg.

History of Dearborn and Ohio Counties, Indiana. Chicago: F.E. Weakley, 1885.

House, Susan Leigh. "Theodore F. Rose Well House." Society of Architectural Historians. https://sah-archipedia.org/buildings/01-105-0048.

Indiana Department of Natural Resources. "DNR: Fish & Wildlife: Bobcats." https://www.in.gov.

Indiana Genealogy Trails. "Dearborn County Indiana History." http://genealogytrails.com/ind/dearborn/history.html.

Indiana Historical Society. "Moores Hill Male and Female College Advertisement." https://images.indianahistory.org.

Indianapolis Star. "Carter Confesses Agrue Slayings." May 21, 1941. https://www.newspapers.com.

———. "June 9, 1924 (Page 6 of 20)." June 9, 1924. https://www.proquest.com.

Indiana University. "William Tinsley Family Journal, 1837–1920." Archives Online at Indiana University. https://webapp1.dlib.indiana.edu/findingaids/welcome.do.

IndyStar. "Unconfirmed Big Cat Sightings Continue around Indiana." February 3, 2014. https://www.indystar.com.

Journal of the Siam Society 4 (1907). https://play.google.com/books/reader?id=JwcWAAAAYAAJ&pg=GBS.PP6&hl=en.

Lawrenceburg (IN) Press. "Of All Things." September 19, 1957.

———. "New County Jail Again Requested by Welfare Head." June 24, 1954.

Lewis and Clark National Historic Trail Experience. "Great Crescent Brewery." https://lewisandclark.travel.

Library of Congress. "Panic of 1937." https://www.americaslibrary.gov/aa/buren/aa_buren_panic_2_e.html.

Linton (IN) Daily Citizen. "Trial of Carter Will Go to Jury." October 21, 1941. https://www.newspapers.com.

Madison County Sheriff. "Dearborn County, IN Jail Inmates Search, Visitation Rules." https://madisoncounty-sheriff.com.

Main Street Aurora. "Suttons Star." *Facebook*, November 8, 2019. https://www.facebook.com/.

Mattingly, Chandra L. "St John Church Celebrates 150 Years." *Dearborn County Register* (Lawrenceburg, IN), March 4, 2010.

Mulroy, Clella. "Driftwood." *Dearborn County Register* (Lawrenceburg, IN), October 25, 1956. https://www.newspapers.com.

Muncie (IN) Evening Press. "Jury Selection in Dink Carter Trial." October 14, 1941. https://www.newspapers.com.

———. "Seek Chair for Slayer of Five." October 14, 1941. https://www.newspapers.com.

National Register of Historic Places Registration Form. "Thomas Gaff House (Hillforest)." Completed April 8, 1992. https://npgallery.nps.gov.

News Staff. "History of Botched Escape Attempt Surfaces with Old Jail Photograph." *Register Publications*, July 7, 2022. https://www.registerpublications.com.

———. "Moores Hill Elementary Is Closing." *Register Publications*, February 23, 2021. https://www.registerpublications.com.

Perleberg, Mike. "Applewood Closing; Road Project Hurt Business." *Eagle Country, 99.3*, November 5, 2013. https://www.eaglecountryonline.com.

———. "South Dearborn Board Won't Close School…Yet." *Eagle 99.3 News*, July 8, 2015. https://www.eaglecountryonline.com.

Pershing, Edgar J. "Lost Battalion of the Revolutionary War, Pa." *National Genealogical Society Quarterly* 16, no. 3, (September 1928): 44–51. https://www.fishergenes.com/showmedia.php?mediaID=100&medialinkID=106.

Putnam Republican Banner (Greencastle, IN). "Spotted Fever." March 8, 1866.

River View Cemetery. "Scenic Beauty. Peaceful Sanctuary." http://aurorariverviewcemetery.com/index.html

Schladen, Marty. "New Jail Will Quadruple Inmate Capacity." *Dearborn County Register* (Lawrenceburg, IN), April 5, 1990. https://www.newspapers.com.

Slayback, Lynn. "Dearborn County Historical Society Post." Dearborn County Historical Society, Facebook. June 29, 2021. https://www.facebook.com.

"Son-In-Law 'Dink' Carter Confesses to Killing Family." *Doorway to History*, May–June 2011. https://www.scribd.com.

St. Mary's Aurora. "History." Accessed December 28, 2022. https://www.stmaryscc.org/history.

Swartz, Tim. "An Unnatural History of Indiana: Out of Place Cats." *Strange Magazine* no. 21, Fall 2020. http://strangemag.com.

Thayer, Travis. "Dearborn Co. Historical Society Shares 1937 Flood Photos You May Have Never Seen." *Eagle Country 99.3*. August 31, 2022. www.eaglecountryonline.com.

The Times (Muncie, IN). "Dink Carter to Die in Chair for Slaying Five." February 9, 1942. https://www.newspapers.com.

Tipton (IN) Daily Tribune. "Murder Case." October 21, 1941. https://www.newspapers.com.

True Northerner (Paw Paw, MI). "A Years' Crimes. August." January 5, 1887.

Wikipedia. "Hillforest." May 30, 2022. https://en.wikipedia.org/wiki/Hillforest.

———. "Kasha (folklore)." December 31, 2022. https://en.wikipedia.org/wiki/Kasha_(folklore).

WikiTree. "Virginius Carter (1908–1942)." https://www.wikitree.com/wiki/Carter-40578.

Wilhelm, Rebecca D., and Hope E. Wilhelm. Interview with Hillforest Staff. Podcast. *Hoosier Myths and Legends Podcast*. Season 1, Episode 15, October 26, 2020.

Wilkymacky, Cathy. "Ghosts, Here?" *Aurora Public Library District Blog*. October 13, 2017. https://eapld.org/2017/10/13/ghosts-here/.

Wood, Korrinn. "Abandoned Mansion from the 1850's." YouTube, June 27, 2020. https://www.youtube.com.

Yesterday's America. "Five Forgotten Locals of Aurora, Indiana." November 12, 2022. https://yesterdaysamerica.com.

ABOUT THE AUTHORS

REBECCA D. WILHELM was born and raised in Hammond, Indiana. She graduated from Hammond High School and continued her education at Vincennes University and St. Mary of the Woods College with a Bachelor of Arts in English. Rebecca is an English Language Arts and Film Literature teacher at Milan High School in Milan, Indiana. She is also the writer and co-host of the podcast *Hoosier Myths and Legends*. Rebecca currently resides in Aurora, Indiana, with her husband, Earl, and their two children, Earl George and Hope.

MARY ELLEN QUIGLEY is a proud Hoosier who was born and raised in Hammond, Indiana. She is a graduate of Marian University, as well as Calumet College of St. Joseph, and is currently pursuing a master's degree from Indiana Wesleyan University. Mary Ellen works as a director of revenue strategy for a hotel management company. When not playing with numbers and spreadsheets all day, she can be found writing romance novels under the pen name M.E. Lavern. She also co-hosts the *Hoosier Myths and Legends* podcast with her sister and niece. Mary Ellen resides in Hebron, Indiana, with her dog, Rudy.

FREE eBOOK OFFER

Scan the QR code below, enter your e-mail address and get our original Haunted America compilation eBook delivered straight to your inbox for free.

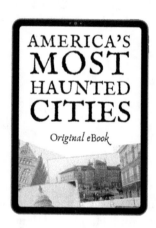

ABOUT THE BOOK

Every city, town, parish, community and school has their own paranormal history. Whether they are spirits caught in the Bardo, ancestors checking on their descendants, restless souls sending a message or simply spectral troublemakers, ghosts have been part of the human tradition from the beginning of time.

In this book, we feature a collection of stories from five of America's most haunted cities: Baltimore, Chicago, Galveston, New Orleans and Washington, D.C.

SCAN TO GET
AMERICA'S MOST HAUNTED CITIES

Having trouble scanning? Go to:
biz.arcadiapublishing.com/americas-most-haunted-cities

Printed in the USA
CPSIA information can be obtained
at www.ICGtesting.com
LVHW011352061023
760261LV00006B/416

9 781540 258038